Kentucky

JUDAIC STUDIES SERIES

Leon J. Weinberger, General Editor

I. J. Schwartz, ca. 1935
Courtesy of YIVO
Institute for Jewish Research

Kentucky

by I. J. Schwartz

Translated by
Gertrude W. Dubrovsky

The University of Alabama Press
Tuscaloosa and London

Copyright © 1990 by
The University of Alabama Press
Tuscaloosa, Alabama 35487–0380
All rights reserved
Manufactured in the United States of America

∞

The paper on which this book is printed meets the minimum re-
quirements of American National Standard for Information Science-
Permanence of Paper for Printed Library Materials, ANSI A39–1984.

Library of Congress Cataloging-in-Publication Data

Schwartz, Israel Jacob, 1885–1971.
　　[Kentoki. English]
　　Kentucky / by I. J. Schwartz ; translated by Gertrude Wishnick
Dubrovsky.
　　　　p.　cm. — (Judaica studies series)
　　Translation of: Kentoki.
　　Includes bibliographical references.
　　ISBN 0-8173-0493-2 (alk. paper)
　　1. Jews—Kentucky—Poetry.　2. Kentucky—Poetry.　I. Dubrovsky,
Gertrude Wishnick, 1926– .　II. Title.　III. Series: Judaica
studies series (Unnumbered)
PJ5129.S298K413　　1990
839'.0913—dc20　　　　　　　　　　　　　　　　　90-10740
　　　　　　　　　　　　　　　　　　　　　　　　　CIP

British Library Cataloguing-in-Publication Data available

I dedicate this book to generations
past, present, and future:

To my parents,
Rose and Benjamin Wishnick,
with whom it all began.

To my sons and daughters-in-law,
Richard and Leora, Steven and Linda,
and Benjamin,
on whom so much depends.

To my grandchildren,
Mairov, Zivthan, Marc, and Ilana,
who must bear the weight of all the generations.

Contents

Translator's Preface

*E*very translator knows the problems of replacing the text of one language with the text of another. While there are universal aspects of human experience, the words to describe that experience are often culture bound. Thus, translation from any language presents problems of both a linguistic and a sociological nature.

If there are problems in translating prose, there are even more in translating poetry. Poetry, a blend of form and meaning, can never be restated, even in the same language, and remain the same. Frost has quite correctly noted that poetry is "that which gets lost in translation." Regardless of the skill and integrity of the translator, there is loss and mutation, and something different emerges. Yet, it is possible, as Stanley Burnshaw has demonstrated in *The Poem Itself*, to introduce a reader to foreign poetry by remaining faithful to the original meaning of the poet. In this translation, I made a commitment to Schwartz's meaning which I could best present by a literal line-by-line translation. I tried to be faithful to Schwartz's lines, to his images where possible, and to his arrangement of details, by which meaning also is carried.* I did not impose on the translation a rhythmic pattern which would have been mine rather than the poet's. Nor did I edit out what some might consider superfluous lines. *Kentucky* must stand on its own merits.

Schwartz's metric scheme is based on a syllabic count. He is rigid in maintaining a line that only occasionally deviates from ten syllables. With the exception of the dedication and the lyric "Kentucky," which have a definite rhyme scheme, and "The Silk Shirt," written in couplets for comic effect, the poems are all in blank verse. Within the lines there are alliterative devices and internal rhymes. These are lost in the translation.

In some instances, the order of the lines had to be changed to make the translation conform to standard American usage. However, this should not present too great a problem to those who wish to read the translation side-by-side with the original.

I have transliterated according to the Yivo system, with the following exceptions: "Kentucky" is rendered in its American form rather than the transliterated "Kentoki." Where there are accepted English spellings of names, I have used them, relying upon the Library of Congress Card Catalog as a guide. Where there are no entries for a writer, I have transliterated from the Yiddish. Where there is a bilingual title for a book, a journal, or a newspaper, I cite the English version given. I have transliterated, rather than translated, Yiddish titles for articles in journals and newspapers because this is the practice when other foreign language articles are cited.

I have used the Yivo system in the case of upper and lower case letters in titles. Only the first word and proper nouns in titles are capitalized.

My model for a Yiddish bibliography was *Yiddish Language and Folklore: A Selective Bibliography for Research* by Uriel and Beatrice Weinreich (The Hague, Netherlands: Mouton & Co., 1959).

---

*Stanley Burnshaw, *The Poem Itself,* (Schocken Books: New York, 1970).

Acknowledgments

S ave for the lonely mountain climber and those others who must face singular challenges, few accomplish tasks totally unaided. Nor did I. Thus, I wish to thank all of those who helped me in this work.

I wish first to express my appreciation to the YIVO Institute for Jewish Research where I had access to its library, its valuable archive collection, and to its staff of trained scholars. I want to particularly thank Rachel Erlich of YIVO, who scrupulously checked and rechecked my translation for accuracy. Her insistence that Schwartz's meaning superseded my poetic license became my *modus operandi*. In addition, at YIVO's Max Weinreich Center for Advanced Jewish Studies, I was able to take courses in Yiddish literature not available elsewhere. Finally, when I needed funds, financial help in the form of a Fellowship Grant was given to me. I also received a grant, gratefully acknowledged, from the Memorial Foundation for Jewish Culture. Thanks also to Dr. Marvin Herzog of YIVO and Columbia University. He was a consistent and important supporter.

There were many individuals who were very helpful to me and to whom I owe more than thanks. Some have passed on, but I wish to remember them in this way. Isaac Dubrovsky, my father-in-law, delighted in my interest in Yiddish literature and took great pride in my work. His encouragement came at a time when I most needed it. My stepmother, Hilda Wishnick, was another person who provided help so that I could work on *Kentucky*. I hope the translation justifies the faith they had in it.

My son Benjamin has been one of my most stalwart champions—in this and many other projects. He and my nephew Bennett Siegel accompanied me on a trip to Kentucky and helped me to see and understand things in a very special way.

Edward Kessler, a friend, a poet, and a scholar, read the entire manuscript and made many valuable and helpful suggestions. Lillis Caulton patiently typed and retyped. Other friends, Linda Oppenheim, Nora Kim, Hannah Fox, Betty Travers, Fanny Peczenik, helped by reading, listening, and discussing *Kentucky* with me. From each I learned something.

Finally, I want to thank my husband Sidney Gray for being there when I needed him.

Gertrude W. Dubrovsky

Kentucky

Introduction

*K*entucky is the major work of the Yiddish poet I. J. Schwartz. Although the book and the poet are almost totally unknown to American audiences, *Kentucky* is one of the most American works in Yiddish literature and is pivotal in what has come to be called Yiddish American literature, that written in Yiddish about the United States. It is the first such work to deal extensively with the American scene, its landscape, history, and people.

Written between 1918 and 1922, *Kentucky* was initially published in chapters in the Yiddish journal *Zukunft* and issued as a book in 1925. It had an immediate effect on Yiddish readers and poets. At a time when most of America's Jews were crowded into the ghettoes of New York City, Schwartz's vision of the rural United States as a home for Jewish settlement extended the horizon for his readers. As he relates the story of Jews who left the cities and dispersed throughout the country, he also tells how the immigrants accepted the challenge of America, how they internalized its values, and how they experienced its problems.

A newcomer to America himself, not steeped in American history, Schwartz wrote about the Kentucky he saw, capturing some sense of the Jewish experience in a strange and exotic new world. *Zukunft* readers in New York who knew only the city streets on which they lived and worked, learned from his poems about the beauty of the interior landscape and something of its history. Schwartz brought new faces, figures, and characters into Yiddish poetry. He acquainted his reading public with rural Christians, pioneers, farmers, even outlaws. He tried to give his immigrant readers some sense of the drama of America as he viewed it.

However, Schwartz is essentially a poet, not a historian. As a poet, he is more interested in the emotional climate which precipitated events rather than the literal truth. In his portrayal of the South after the Civil War, there are inevitably some factual errors. For example, Daniel Boone was not the first "to see the land of blue grass." And while Kentucky is not really the "far South," but a border state very different from Mississippi, Alabama, or Georgia, it was as far south as Schwartz traveled at that time, and a universe away from the America of New York City. Yet, in spite of his taking poetic license, he accurately reflects an immigrant experience not easily found in other sources.

The poet's focus is on those immigrants who ventured out of the cities in which they landed, and searched for the America about which they had dreamed. In contrast to the closed insular European *shtetl*[1] of the old world and the oppressive city ghetto of the new, the sensuous panorama of the Blue Grass country as Schwartz painted it opened America and animated the imaginations of readers who saw in *Kentucky* another life option.[2]

Potential immigrants, many of whom studied *Kentucky* in their schools in such remote places as Vilna, Poland, and Buenos Aires, Argentina, received their first impressions of America through these poems. The impact was further strengthened when portions were set to music and sung in Yiddish choruses around the world. For the readers and listeners, Kentucky became a symbol of all that was fruitful and exotic in the New World to which they aspired.

I

American literature is derived from as many languages as there are cultures. The creative works of immigrant writers provide a rich record of their reactions to and experiences in the diverse communities where they settled. The Eastern European Jews added their Yiddish voice to that body of American literature which grows out of the encounter with the New World.

Yiddish-American literature had its beginnings in the 1880s, almost as soon as significant numbers of Yiddish speakers arrived on our shores. It is still being created. For example, Isaac Bashevis Singer, whose Nobel Prize makes him the most famous of contemporary Yiddish writers, continues to publish serialized novels in the Yiddish newspaper *Forward*. Ironically, however, Singer's work is immediately translated into English, and his books, for the most part, are not available in Yiddish.

The sad fact is that there are not enough Yiddish readers left to sustain the publication and insure the continuation of a lively Yiddish literature in the country. Before World War II, America provided fertile ground for an outpouring of creative energy which resulted in an exuberant flowering of all kinds of artistic works. But, the destruction of the Eastern European Jewish community, where Yiddish was the primary language, effectively caused an end to them. No new Yiddish speaking immigrants are arriving here, or anywhere else, to bolster and reinforce the language. It remains, like the memory of the flavors and aromas of childhood, in the background consciousness of second and third generation Jews in America, and then disappears.

However, in the first half of this century, Yiddish writers and artists and other Jewish immigrants explored the American scene which impressed itself on their sensibilities. Within their capabilities they contributed to American literature, art, agriculture, industry, economics, science and technology.

In his Introduction to the *Literary History of the United States,* Spiller defines American literature as "the record and analysis of a series of cultural waves beating in from across the Atlantic to our shores in an continuous series and changing their form and nature, and sometimes their direction as they sweep over the New World." He points out that American literature incorporates two themes: an old literary theme of "cutting loose and faring forth," and the theme of "nostalgia for the rich culture of Europe" which was irrevocably left behind.[3]

The two themes, the looking backward, and the journeying forwards are also found in Yiddish American literature, which evolved in the same way as the rest but at a much faster pace.

In the 1880s, popular Yiddish literature in America was full of nostalgia for the home left behind. Show tunes and songs such as *a brivele der mamen* [A Letter to Mother] and *di mames entfer* [The Mother's Answer] reflect a longing for the past and the pain of the separation.

Joseph Opatoshu, writing of this period, feels that the social and economic environment which the nineteenth-century Jewish immigrants found here did not encourage the development of a more optimistic literature: "Jewish life [in America] was too turbulent, too confused. There was no tranquility. . . . There were no roots, no ancestors."[4]

Driven by desperate poverty, feeling unable to establish themselves, developing no affection for America, indeed critical of all things American, many of the turn-of-the-century immigrants thought of this country as an interlude in their lives. Their most cherished dream was to save enough money to return to Europe. Disappointed and despairing of any future, they looked back on the past in their songs and their poetry.

Yet, almost simultaneously, a more forward looking literature was developing. In the 1890s radical writers such as Morris Winchevsky,

3

David Edelstadt, Joseph Bovshover, and Morris Rosenfeld voiced fresh concerns for the Jews in America. Joining the new labor movement to help improve working conditions, these poets, who themselves labored in sweatshops and lived in crowded tenements, wrote of their experiences in starkly realistic poems and stories in which the social message was very clear. Some of their lyrics, particularly those of Rosenfeld, were sung or recited at union meetings to urge Jewish workers to join the picket lines and fight for economic justice.

After the failure of the Russian revolution in 1905, another wave of Jewish immigrants arrived in America. Burning their bridges behind them, the new arrivals no longer dreamed of returning to "the old home," but were determined to make the new country a new home. In their writing, we find the theme of "cutting loose and faring forth"[5] clearly expressed. They sounded the theme of America as a land of unending opportunity, took real pleasure and joy in the American landscape, and found renewed hope for the future.

Among those who arrived in the years between 1905 and 1910 was a gifted group of young poets and writers. They included Zisha Landau, Reuben Eisland, M. Haimowitz, Mani Leib, H. Leivick, M. L. Halperin, I. J. Schwartz, and others. Settling in New York like most of their coreligionists, they first met each other in the factories, cafes, and streets of the city. Discovering that they were united by a common interest in poetry and aesthetics, they formed a literary group which had a far-reaching impact on Yiddish literature, impelling it on a course towards modernism. Because of their youth and their enthusiasm, they were given the name *di yunge* [the young ones] by Leivick.

Di yunge, influenced by the impressionists in art and the symbolists in literature, tried to create an aesthetic theory as a framework for their art. They were contemptuous of the nostalgia, sentimentality, and triteness of popular Yiddish literature at that time, and scornful of the moralizing tone of the realistic predecessors, the sweatshop and labor poets. They saw both styles as being inconsistent with the function of art. Art, they felt, does not have to educate or guide Jewish workers. Instead, artistic form and literary expression must give beauty and sparkle to folk life, and portray the moods, feelings, hopes, and joys of the Jews.

Di yunge wanted to celebrated the new American scene as they saw it, and in an art form that was primarily the expression of the unique sensitivity and individual mood of the artist. Like the European impressionists, they regarded themselves as painters in words who hoped to capture each fleeting moment of time before it dissolved completely in the rapid whirl of events. Instead of attempting to reform social conditions, they tried to create sensuous images and tonal effects. Their emphasis in 1907 on the use of images to portray a singular feeling was

4

remarkably similar to that of the Imagists, whose credo was published in 1915 by Amy Lowell in a preface to *Some Imagist Poets*. However, neither Amy Lowell, nor any of the Imagists, knew of *di yunge,* nor is it likely that *di yunge* knew of the Imagists.

New thrusts of energy were set in motion by the contact of these young poets and writers with their new country. Their first publication, *Jugend,* which came out in only three issues in 1907–1908, reflects not only new artistic impulses in form and style, but also entirely new themes in Yiddish literature. They write of the existential search for meaning in a world devoid of hope; they are interested in the power of sexual fantasies, incestuous feelings, anxieties, guilt, and romantic love; and they write about nature in a new and personal way.

In concentrating on their new American home, some inevitably wrote of their unhappy experiences in the shops and tenements of New York. Others, animated by the seemingly boundless possibilities of America, travelled outside the limits of New York City to regions south and west of the Hudson, and were enthralled by the country stretching out in front of them. Isaac Raboy, a novelist, moved to a farm in the Dakotas and wrote the first Yiddish western, *Herr Goldenbarg,* in 1916. Peretz Hirschbein, a dramatist, took an extended tour of America and wrote the first Yiddish American travelogue, *America,* in 1918. In the same year, I. J. Schwartz left for Lexington, Kentucky. His book *Kentucky* grew out of his Southern experiences.

II

Israel Jacob Schwartz was born in the little Lithuanian town of Petrushani in the province of Kovno.[6] Zalman Reisin's *Liksikon fun der yidisher literatur* (1929) gives his birthdate according to the Jewish calendar: Sukkoth, 1885. In the YIVO library copy of the *Liksikon,* the date of his death has been added in ink, 9/19/71. The difference between the dates—the Jewish calendar date to mark the beginning and the Roman to mark the ending—tells, in microcosm, Schwartz's story. Born into an orthodox religious home in Lithuania, he died areligious—if not agnostic—in New York. Yet, the influence of his childhood religious education and training never really left him and his poetry is full of biblical allusions from his early reading.

Schwartz was the second son of an orthodox rabbi, Yitzkhok Schwartz, from whom he received a scrupulous religious education at home. At a young age, he was sent to a Yeshiva in Kovno to continue his religious studies. Here, he came under the influence of the Haskalah, the Jewish Enlightenment,[7] and became familiar with secular Russian,

5

Polish, and Hebrew literature. Upon his arrival in America in 1906, he enrolled in a high school and mastered the language well enough to read and translate English and American writers.

Like many immigrants, Schwartz emigrated for a combination of reasons. Political and economic pressures played a large part in his painful decision to leave his home. He himself said he came three years after a terrible pogrom: "A Christian rock thrown at a Jewish head drove me here."[8] In addition, he had relatives in America—a married sister and a brother, Abraham S. Schwartz, a poet also and studying to become a doctor.

However, like that of most of the émigrés, Schwartz's parting from his European home and from his parents to whom he was devoted was extremely painful for him, and he carried that pain with him to the end of his days. In an autobiographical poem, "Parting," published in 1951, he described his departure (see Appendix). It begins: "The picture of my final parting from home / Rises up before me with all its anguish / And excruciating pain." For Schwartz, writing was the way to quiet his longing for his old home, and to identify with his new one.

The new country stretched the young poet's imagination. It was an adventure, a quest, a discovery, a place of infinite possibility. He told the Yiddish writer Jacob Pat: "The world here, in America, was young, unknown, frightening, like the first seven days of creation. We came into the new land and fires were lit in our veins with the first few steps."[9]

America, for I. J. Schwartz, was the start of a journey, the excitement of which continued throughout his life. It originated in Lithuania, took him across Europe, across the ocean, and deposited him in New York, which he thought of as a new beginning. His poem "Blue Grass" tells of his initial reaction to the city he grew to love.

From New York, he, his wife, Mary, and daughter, Sylvia, moved in 1918 to Lexington, Kentucky, at the suggestion of his married sister, Lena Krasne, who settled there with her husband, Samuel, in 1904. Once settled, Schwartz and his wife opened the New York Wholesale Millinery which also sold ready-to-wear clothing for women and children. His wife managed the store; Schwartz worked with her, and spent his evenings writing. He made regular buying trips to New York, then the garment center of the world, to order stock. The trips also were important for the opportunity they afforded him to visit with the Yiddish literati and to share his writing with them. Evidently, the business succeeded enough for the Schwartzes to have a summer cottage at the river beach near Boonesboro, a few miles from Lexington.[10] After twelve years, the family left Kentucky and moved to Florida, to New Mexico, and to points even farther West. When he sensed that his journey was drawing to a close, Schwartz came back to New York, the place where it started. "It was here that the journey began," he said, "and it is here where it must end."[11]

The movement and journeying which characterized *Kentucky* is a reflection of its author's life. Joshua, of "New Earth," moves both horizontally and vertically. Literally, he has come after a long hard journey across sea and land—from East to West, from North to South—before settling in one place. Metaphorically, he begins moving up the ladder of success, moving with his aspirations higher and higher, outdistancing the neighbors who had been rooted in the area for generations. It is, in effect, Schwartz's story.

Like the narrator of the opening poem in *Kentucky*, Schwartz felt himself to be a bridge between two worlds: that of his past, his and his parents' world; and that of the future, his own child's. He contained the two within himself, but he was, at the same time, somehow apart from both. He was destined to be essentially rootless, continually on the move, continually observing and being enlarged by the life around him. From his peculiar and isolated position of wanderer and observer, he could appreciate the contrast between the naive simplicity of provincials and the complexity of one who has walked alone on the country roads and city streets of America.

Although Schwartz felt himself to be on the margin of American society, he was, nevertheless, involved with contemporaries. They provide a picture of the poet as a quiet, gentle man who loved to laugh and yet was serious, a man who participated in various adventures with gusto, and still had a core of serenity. Tall and handsome with dark curly hair and an imposing physique, Schwartz delighted especially in the company of women. As a young man, he was constantly joking, quipping, and punning. One writer describes him as follows: "He loved life, and like a youth released from school, he gamboled freely. And yet, he would not foolishly waste his time. He knew the world's great thinkers; he could still join a congregation in a synagogue; his soft eyes were always dreaming."[12]

Associated with the *Yunge* from the beginning of his arrival in New York, Schwartz enjoyed their friendship, but did not get enmeshed in the bitterness of the literary battle inspired by their aesthetic revolt. He saw how the battle drained the creative energy from the contenders. The writer Reuben Eisland points out that "in contrast to most of the *Yunge* who are cheerless and bad humored, [Schwartz] is alsmost always happy and full of *joie de vivre*."[13] Another critic, A. Mukdani, also contrasts Schwartz to the *Yunge*: "He was the quietest poet among the *Yunge*. He made no revolutions, which was the rule for the Yiddish poets in the early part of the century. He organized no poetic circles of fighters or agitators, founded no new poetic creeds, theories, or schools. He had a Sabbath peace around himself which is found in his poetry."[14]

Quiet though he might have been, Schwartz, absorbed and experimented with new poetic ideas which excited his friends. The *Yunge* generally tried to capture the sense impressions of a scene, and their poetry is full of sensuous imagery. Schwartz found in nature the perfect object to engage all his senses. Thus, it becomes a real presence in his poetry. Years later, shortly before he died, the poet, reflecting on his work, expressed concern that he might have "overdone with smells and with . . . giving nature such a say."[15] Yet, his rhapsodic response is genuine. Of all the *Yunge,* he is reputed to be the only one "who possesses a real feeling for nature,"[16] devoid of any pretentions or posturing.

Schwartz's poetic debut occurred before his arrival in America. His translation of Chaim Nachman Bialik's *"In Feld,"* and an original lyrical poem by Schwartz, *"Blumen,"* appeared in an anthology published in Vilna in 1906.[17] Subsequently, he translated almost all of Bialik's Hebrew poetry into Yiddish and his fame depends almost as much on his abilities as a translator as on his original poetry.

In addition, Schwartz translated into Yiddish the Spanish Sephardic poetry of the Middle Ages. From English literature, he translated parts of Milton's "Paradise Lost," Shakespearean sonnets, and two plays, "Hamlet" and "Julius Caesar." From American literature, Schwartz translated from his favorite poet and the one who, by his admission, had the greatest influence on him—Walt Whitman.[18] His translation of Whitman's "Salud au Monde" appears in *Shriften,* a 1912 publication of the *Yunge.*

To Schwartz, Whitman was *the* American poet, epitomizing what was best in American writing, and his influence is apparent in almost every section of *Kentucky.* Schwartz's sensuous responses to nature, his ability to observe a whole landscape and to evoke a personal response to the scene is Whitman's. In an interview, Schwartz says, "I read Walt Whitman very much. I translated some poems of Whitman's . . . He is a great poet . . . Whitman is writing nothing but the American scene. But to me, it would have been the same thing if he had written about the English scene or the European one . . . He is open. And you feel that he says what he wants to say. Open. Free. Generous. That's Walt Whitman."[19] Perhaps Schwartz intended a compliment to Whitman by the opening words of "New Earth": "Wide, open, free lay the land."

According to the Yiddish poet and critic, Aaron Glants-Leyeliss, *Kentucky* was Schwartz's way of making Whitman's land his own: "An earth, a soil, especially when one starts to step on it in the years of comparative ripeness—then it becomes one's own, when one sees the landscape and one starts to paint it. Until that happens, one is relatively a stranger, an immigrant with the whole package of immigrant psychology on his shoulders and in his soul. Even citizen papers do not help. Sensing the landscape, seeing her colors, catching her aromas, this is what making the land one's own means—making it a new home."[20]

If Schwartz did not quite succeed in making the land his own, he did "paint" the scene and "catch the aromas." Somehow, the poet from Lithuania was able to absorb the South he viewed: its landscape, its undercurrents of change, its divisive tensions, its whole bloody history. "He went to Lexington to seek a living," comments Mukdani, "and instead wrote the first important work in Yiddish literature in America."[21]

III

Kentucky is a book of nine poems which gives both an immigrant's impression of the South "after the Civil War," and the reaction of a poet to a new life experience for Jewish immigrants in America. They are written in blank verse; Schwartz's metric system depends on a decasyllabic line. The poems can be placed into four groups as follows:

Group I.	Dedication
	Blue Grass
Group II.	New Earth
Group III.	John
	Joe
	George Washington
	The Silk Shirt
Group IV.	Kentucky
	The End of Thomas

The dedicatory poem and "Blue Grass" are personal poems related to the poet's life and feelings. They serve as a frame for the collection and establish a point of reference for the narrative.

"New Earth" is the heart of the book, comprising two thirds of the entire text in the original Yiddish. In the figure of its protagonist, Joshua, we get an extended picture of a New World personality. The poet traces Joshua's migration from Europe to New York, and from New York to Lexington where he moved up the ladder from peddler to an economic power known throughout the South. The story is taken through three generations; the history of the single family is a microcosm of Jewish immigrants in rural America and their ultimate Americanization and acculturation.

The other poems are related Southern sketches and introduce characters new to Schwartz—feuding mountaineers and moonshiners, proud Anglo-Saxons, rural Christians, oppressed and hounded blacks—

as well as a young Jew who marries a Christian and is destroyed by his new relatives. This group represents the new America, "the forging of a new culture on the plains of Kentucky, from European and African elements."[22]

Finally, in the last two poems, "Kentucky" and "The End of Thomas," the poet focusses on what is wrong in the new Garden of Eden he has encountered, the evil that must be contained lest we are all doomed.

Wanting to present all facets of the Southern experience fairly, Schwartz consciously tries to achieve a balance in his collection. The portrayal of a Jewish family is balanced by that of a Black family. We have a story, "Joe," about a young Jewish immigrant, and another, "John," a young Christian hillbilly, both of whom die violently. We then have two stories about young blacks, "George Washington" and "Thomas." Finally, the first two poems, the untitled "Dedication" and "Blue Grass," which envision the dream of the new land, the new home, are structurally balanced by the lyric "Kentucky" and "The End of Thomas," which reveal the contradictions in the dream.

In many ways, *Kentucky* is a collection of morality tales deriving from a tradition of Hebrew and Yiddish literature. Behind it is the language and the melody of the Old Testament. Joshua, of "New Earth," settles in what the poet calls "the new land Canaan" after years of wandering, just as the biblical prototype does. Schwartz lifts whole passages out of the Bible: Joshua begs his Christian neighbors for a burial place for his child in almost the same words with which Abraham begs the foreign Hittites for a burial place for Sarah, his wife; Joshua's dream in the Christian's barn is Jacob's dream, given an ironic twist.

In addition to the biblical source, *Kentucky* also draws from European and American writers. The epic form of "New Earth" grows out of an old European tradition of epic poetry used by such Yiddish writers as Peretz, Kulback, Shteynberg, Boraisha, and others, and such American writers as Henry Wadsworth Longfellow and Walt Whitman.

In its broadest sense, the epic deals with society, nature, philosophy, and history. It was considered an important vehicle for passing on values of a particular group. Traditionally, the epic hero represents the group at its best and helps society understand the distance between normal humanity and humanity at its most heroic. But Schwartz's hero grows smaller rather than larger during the course of his epic as the poet pictures failure, rather than success, on a large scale: the Civil War failed to free people; America failed to provide a secure home for Judaism; and Joshua, assuming the wrong values of his new country, fails himself, his family, and his faith. Schwartz's epic hero ends materially wealthy, but considerably diminished spiritually.

Yet, the epic sweep gives "New Earth" a dignity, as the poet traces a family through three generations and records its growth, like a set of nesting blocks: the family grows; the Jewish community develops around it; the city expands and flourishes. It is the first Yiddish epic to attempt so comprehensive a view.

Schwartz acknowledged Longfellow as one of the American influences on *Kentucky*.[23] In depicting the lives of ethnic, religious, or regional groups, Longfellow reverts to the older European epic tradition. "Evangeline" is the story of exiled Canadian villagers; "Hiawatha" concerns the American Indian; "The Courtship of Miles Standish" is about a New England community. Like Longfellow, Schwartz writes about specific ethnic communities: Jewish immigrants (German and Lithuanian), mountain people, Blacks. His poem "The End of Thomas" comes directly from Longfellow's "The Slave in the Dismal Swamp."

According to Schwartz's own testimony, his greatest American influence was Walt Whitman, whose *Leaves of Grass* has been called the national epic of America.[24] Structurally, *Kentucky* is similar to *Leaves of Grass*. As Whitman explores the American landscape and himself in the midst of it, trying to make sense of both, so, too, does Schwartz explore the Southern landscape of Kentucky and himself in relationship to his new home. Where Whitman establishes the identity of the self as the modern man in "Song of Myself," Schwartz establishes the identity of the narrator—the participant-observer—in his "Dedication" and "Blue Grass." Whitman elaborates on the New World man who is both unique and typical, a person alone yet in society with others. In "New Earth," Schwartz introduces his New World personality, Joshua, who exemplifies the Whitman hero. Joshua experiences his personal anxieties, joys, and sorrows; but, at the same time, he typifies the thousands of immigrants who landed in New York and were not able to adjust to the city. With peddler's packs, they started out across America in search of a better life. "New Earth" provides an extended picture of the life and death of this new American. John, Joe, George Washington, and Tom are other Southern personalities with whom the New World man must live.

The black section of *Kentucky* contains the story of Thomas and reveals the national crisis as Schwartz perceived it. Whitman's epic hero, searching for spiritual fulfillment, engages in the Civil War, a struggle on which the national destiny depends. In Kentucky, Thomas fights a losing battle against a lynch mob. Not only is his personal fate involved, but the national destiny symbolically depends on the outcome. Thomas, looking for spiritual answers, realizes that his fate is inextricably tied to his black skin. His quest for spiritual fulfillment is suspended as Schwartz asks the ethical question to which there is no rational answer: "How can one man condemn another to death?"

Schwartz writes about the same paradox Whitman expresses in his poem, "This Compost," which pictures the earth as a huge mixture of fertility and decay and "grows such sweet things out of such corruptions." Joshua's first impression of his new home contains the same sense of growth and death as he sees "free stretches of land . . . and humid wild woods" from which comes an "unknown tropical essence of blossoming and decay."

The two major themes linking the separate poems of *Kentucky* are the uncertain future of Jewish immigrants settling in America, and the oppression and victimization of the Black in the South. The themes are developed within the context of the antithesis suggested by the phrase "blossoming and decay," while the phrase itself provides a key to the poet's dual view of the New World and his reaction to its mixed blessings. On the one hand, he glories in the expansiveness, fruitfulness, and opulence of the land he sees in front of him, stretching like a Garden of Eden. On the other hand, he understands some of the tragedy on which the glory rests.

The primary images of *Kentucky* are trees and blood. Trees are associated with growth, productivity, and stability. Blood is associated with injustice, persecution, oppression, and death. It is also ironically associated with fertility and productivity. Through the poems, Schwartz conveys a sense that the flowers of the South have been rooted in blood. Their blossoming becomes both seductive and threatening.

The state, Kentucky, gets its name from an old Indian word whose exact meaning is not known. At one time the region was called The Dark and Bloody Ground because of the fierce battles between the whites and the Indians. Schwartz's original title for "New Earth" was "*Oyfn Blutikn Grunt*"[25] (On the Bloody Ground). In the opening and closing scenes of "New Earth" the Blacks and the Jew are seen together in a red landscape associated with twilight. The color is repeated so often that it is impossible to miss the symbolic significance. It is not only the evening landscape tinted red by rays of the setting sun, but it is a world which has assumed this coloration. Schwartz writes of the bloody Civil War, he touches upon the life and death struggle with the Redman, the blood-feuds which go on for generations and, most sinister of all, the blood extracted from the Blacks.

The ideas of persecution and growth, "blossoming and decay," blood and trees, come together in the figure of the Jew who comes with his own blood-drenched history into the blood-drenched South. Explicitly compared to a transplanted tree engaged in a battle with an inhospitable soil, Joshua takes root and, blossoming, prospers. But his prosperity literally rests on blood. Not only does he deal with bloody hides to earn

12

his living, but the death of his child is a kind of blood sacrifice for his business.

Schwartz understands that the confrontation of the Old World with the New often results in the sacrifice of the specific character of Jewish life. At the same time, the oppression of the Blacks is a constant reminder that whatever else America offers, ultimate security and freedom cannot be assumed. He knows that the Blacks and the Jews have had a similar history of persecution and suffering.

Schwartz, empathizing with the Blacks, identifies so strongly with them that he tends to see them as Jews. Arguments between George Washington and his wife Maggie are embellished with ironic Yiddish curses and sayings; the Black church is like a synagogue where spirituals are sung in Yiddish; a special dinner at a Black home is like the Sabbath meal in a Jewish home.

But, sympathetic as he is, Schwartz offends contemporary sensibilities by his use of stock images to characterize Blacks. Like minstrel caricatures, black bodies and faces glisten and gleam, they grin from ear to ear, their red lips outline their strong white teeth, they roll their eyes so that only the whites show, and so on. Yet, despite this, in 1918, he was among the very few writers in America to use blacks as fully realizable literary figures with whom readers could empathize. In concentrating on their universal human emotions, he created believable characters and sympathetically portrayed their tragicomic lives on earth.[26]

Schwartz had more difficulty describing white Christians who appear as flat, two-dimensional personae. Joseph Jones, in his discussion of Schwartz in Lexington, writes, "The poem about John, the mountaineer in conflict with urban society and the law, is a sort of benevolent tourist's view of the backwoodsman, distorted, if sympathetic, and as parodic as today's television world of the rural South."[27] Schwartz's Christians seem to have no memories of a past to inform their lives; their behavior is determined by primitive passions. He tries to get at the Christian experience; his poem "John" concerns only Christians. But his inability to identify with them makes the piece unconvincing.

Schwartz's restraint in picturing the white Southern Christians and his misgivings about them is directly related to the irrational hatred and injustice he must have observed, and to his own sense of "otherness." He knows that the hostility of the bigot might as easily be directed against the Jew as the Black, and shows as much in the poem "Joe."

In 1915, three years before Schwartz moved to Kentucky, Leo Frank of Georgia was the first Jew ever murdered by a lynch mob in the United States. The case, and the vicious anti-Semitic campaign carried on around

13

it—Frank was repeatedly referred to as "the filthy perverted Jew from New York"[28]—presented dramatic evidence to Schwartz and other Jews that they were not necessarily safe in their new home. Indeed, the anti-Semitism generated by the trial reportedly gave the final impetus to the establishment of the Anti-Defamation League.[29]

Schwartz was certainly not indifferent to the overt signs of oppression and injustice in his new country. Yet, he sees an even greater threat in the destruction of traditional Jewish life through Americanization. In Schwartz's words, the immigrants anticipating their departure knew in Europe what was required of them in America: "In Columbus's country, it is not a sin to work on the Sabbath." They knew that the new country broke a centuries-old pattern in Jewish life, and they made promises to themselves and their relatives that they would keep the traditions alive and meaningful.[30] But the promises started to evaporate with the salt air of the ocean trip.

The story of Joshua shows how the Americanization process often was accompanied by the breakdown of values and lifestyles. As business success assumes an increasingly important place in Joshua's life, religious practices become more and more burdensome until they are totally abandoned. Joshua discards both his peddler's pack and prayer books in the corner of an attic, and no longer observes the Sabbath. His family is irrevocably affected by the substitution of the American dream of success for traditional practices and values. Joshua's wife tries to maintain a Jewish home and becomes an anomaly to her children.

Schwartz sees the Jewish woman as having little control over the lifestyle or destiny of her family. In fact, she has no voice. Only Joshua makes the crucial decisions without consulting his wife. He alone decides on the place where his family will settle, and when he has set down his stakes, he sends for his wife and children to join him. It is he who decides that business obligations supersede Jewish ones. It is at this point that the family starts a spiritual decline.

When Joshua, more and more preoccupied with business, gives up the Sabbath observance and significantly changes a pattern within the family, the wife can only sigh. Not able to argue with her husband, she merely continues to prepare the meal as before, and feels herself growing distant from her husband, her children, and her new home. Silent throughout most of the poem, the wife cries out only at the grave of her young daughter. Lamenting the bitter life she is forced to lead, she voices her fear that the remaining children will be lost to Judaism.

The woman dies as she lived, silent. Her last act is to fix her husband with a gloomy look he finds hard to forget. Even for her funeral, her wishes are ignored. She is dressed in elegant silk, the room in which she is 'laid out' is overflowing with flowers, the service is conducted by a

14

hatless Reform Rabbi, the service and the burial more Christian than Jewish and not at all as she would have wished it.

From the beginning of "New Earth," the poet prepares for the inevitable end of Joshua's family. Yankele and Pearl, the children born elsewhere, are brought to the new land, the new home, and must also face its challenges. Yankele adapts without any difficulty. He soon becomes Jake, a healthy obstreperous youngster who almost immediately starts to "jabber in a strange tongue." And as he studies the "Christian" subjects in school, he abandons completely the Jewish subjects at home. The other child, Pearl, is weak, pale, and ailing. She sits quietly, and observing everything, she sees nothing. Quietly she dies. Like the transplanted Jewish tradition which she may symbolize, she could not withstand the inhospitable pressures of the new home.

"God Takes, God Gives" is how Schwartz titles the chapter following Pearl's death. Here he reverses a biblical phrase. The reversal is significant, for in the context of the whole poem the title of the chapter expresses what Schwartz sees as a bitter cosmic joke. Pearl is replaced by Lionel (dull and fat), Willard (pompous prig), Edwin (incorrigible gambler), Diana (the cliché of the vulgar middle class), Dorothy and Ethel (enigmatic, repressed shadows of women). These American children with their new American names no longer have ties with their past.

Adapting eagerly the current fashions of their Christian friends, the American children grow estranged from the old roots. Southern attitudes solidify, rooted and strengthened in the secular schools which the children attend. "A nigger is a nigger, and that's that!" says the young Jacob to his stupefied parents. Together with his friends, he plays tricks designed to terrify Black children. Among those born in the South, "none needed to be Americanized," notes Schwartz, somewhat sardonically.

It takes a third generation, in the form of David, to be comfortable enough with the family's affluence so that he could be "independent, not avaricious." With the third generation, there is hope for a return to the old values.

IV

Kentucky is a valuable social document and much can be learned from it about the non-urban experience of Jews in America. Jewish immigrants, at the turn of the century, spread out over the whole country, settling in small cities, towns, rural hamlets, and on farms.

At the same time, Jewish farming in America became a theme in the

Yiddish press and in popular Yiddish literature. The Baron De Hirsch had already established the Jewish Agricultural Society which helped immigrant Jews without prior experience in agriculture become farmers. Thus in "New Earth," Joshua's grandson David, symbol of the American child returning to Jewish roots and values, decides to become a farmer. While his mother and uncles are aghast at the idea, his grandfather, who, in his old age, had become miserly, is delighted and provides the financial support David needs. "Oh, what good apples we'll eat," says old Josh in happy anticipation. And the rest of the family reconciled themselves when they saw how positive an effect farming had on David. In the story of Joe, the Jew who did not succeed, we find him living in his uncle's house when he first arrives in America. On the wall hang pictures of "Baron Hirsch and Jacob Schiff," both of whom were influential in the movement towards Jewish agriculture in America. Joe, forced to marry a Christian girl he impregnates, lives on her father's farm and in time his personal trauma and tragedy is alleviated by his new relationship to the land.

Once immigrants settle, they typically write to their friends and relatives extolling the virtues of a particular location and urging them to join. Schwartz, who fictionalizes this experience in the figure of Daniel Boone writing to his relatives, came to Lexington at the invitation of his sister who told him that he could make a living in the South. In this way, Jewish communities in small towns and rural enclaves of America mushroomed. Some became well established, like the one in Lexington, Kentucky; others lasted a period of time and then disappeared. It is difficult to get accurate demographic data and in general most of our social scientists have not examined the movement of Jews from the urban centers to the American interior. Were it not for the Yiddish poets and writers, we would know very little about this aspect of American and immigrant history.

V

Although *Kentucky* offers a valuable glimpse into the American experience of certain of its newcomers, Schwartz is no polemicist, nor is his major work intended as social history.

It is a book of poetry, somewhat uneven in quality. A reader might puzzle over some illogical time sequences, or be disturbed by an inconsistency in tone as passages go from spontaneous lyricism to flat exposition, or be annoyed at excessive modifiers and unnecessary repetitions. Yet, despite these weaknesses, *Kentucky* has considerable poetic powers and a compelling interest.

We are caught up in the archetypal story of Joshua, a wandering Jew

16

who sets down roots and rises to a position of power in a foreign community, while that which makes him what he is erodes. Schwartz writes with a dramatist's eye, painting a setting, sketching a scene, and creating characters who not only act, but think and feel. When Schwartz describes the natural world, he piles detail upon detail until we can almost see, smell, and experience it as he did. He creates realistic dialogue, and his dramatic scenes have an internal tension as the characters seek to resolve conflicts which the reader recognizes as universal. When Jacob's new Christian relative confronts Joshua and Sarah with his anger at a marriage he does not like—Joshua's son and the farmer's niece— we understand the distress of the old couple, reminded as they are of their former impoverished state and accused of "ingratitude" for their new success. As the two cultures try to merge, we see that assimilation has its price. While the poet was enraptured with the new land, he was, at the same time, troubled about the future of both Jews and Judaism in it.

Whitman said of *Leaves of Grass:* "In the midst of all, it gives one man's—the author's—identity, ardors, observations, faiths, and thought." The same can be said of Schwartz's *Kentucky.* As Whitman abandoned conventional themes and sang "quite solely with reference to America," so did Schwartz. He, too, reflected on "themes and things, old and new, in the lights thrown on them by the advent of America and democracy."[31]

The themes Schwartz developed grew out of the questions he puzzled over: How were new American lifestyles and values affecting old ways? How do the immigrants interact with and relate to the people with whom they come in contact? What is wrong in the new Garden of Eden? These are questions which thoughtful newcomers—Puerto Rican, Cuban, Chinese, or other ethnics—ask even today as they try to establish new roots in the Promised Land.

Gertrude W. Dubrovsky

Princeton, New Jersey
July 19, 1989

Notes

[The Yiddish articles cited were translated by the author.]

Introduction

1. Yiddish word for small town, usually referring to the Eastern European community. A large percentage of Eastern European Jewish immigrants came

from small rural communities at the edge of large cities. There, they lived restricted lives: they could only engage in limited occupations and, for the most part, were not permitted to own land. Many became tradesmen, eking out a spare living in the larger towns and cities; but they lived a rural lifestyle.

2. One of the possibilities that America offered was land ownership. An ideological group of young Russian intellectuals in Europe—Am Olam [Eternal People]—actually prepared to become farmers in America. Abraham Kahan, founder and first editor of the Jewish *Forward,* was one of these. However, at his arrival in New York, he found the city so exciting that moving to the countryside became unthinkable for him. But others among the arriving immigrants were greatly disappointed. The city heightened their sense of dislocation and their anguish at the permanent separation from native homes and family. An unknown number left the cities for the interior of the country. If they could not go back home again, they did the next best thing and moved to a more familiar type of environment. The demographic data on this "out-migration" is fragmentary and comparatively little has been written about it. Yet, Yiddish writers, like Schwartz, who made the same exodus, described what they saw and felt. Although these writers were not writing "history" per se, their work, nevertheless, provides a rich source of social history for contemporary readers.

3. Robert Spiller, et al., *Literary History of the United States,* (New York: The Macmillan Co., 1959) p. xx.

4. Joseph Opatoshu, "Fifty Years of Yiddish Literature in the United States," *YIVO Annual of Jewish Social Science,* Vol IX, 1954, pp. 77–78.

5. Spiller, *Literary History,* p. xxii.

6. In 1905, Lithuania was part of Russia.

7. The Haskalah, a movement to end the cultural isolation of European Jews by modernizing and secularizing education and encouraging Jews to adopt the life-style of the surrounding culture, reached Russia about 1860–80, in the years shortly before Schwartz's birth.

8. Jacob Pat, "*Y. Y. Shvartz: tsu zayn 75 yubeley,*" *Di Presse* (November 19, 1961).

9. Pat, "*Y. Y. Shvarts,*" *op. cit.*

10. For details of the life of the Schwartz family in Lexington, see Joseph R. Jones, "I. J. Schwartz in Lexington," *The Kentucky Review,* Volume III, No. 1 (1981) pp. 23–40.

11. These details were supplied by Schwartz. See Gertrude Dubrovsky, *Midstream,* "I. J. Schwartz (1885–1971) In Memoriam," December 1971, pp. 52–57.

12. Israel Blum, "In mayn literarishe akhsanye," *Zukunft* (January, 1961) p. 32.

13. Reuben Eisland, "Di Yunge," *Shriften,* Vol. I (1912) p. 17.

14. A. Mukdani, "Y. Y. Shvarts," *Di goldene keyt,* Vol. 24 (1956) p. 158.

15. Gertrude Dubrovsky, "Between a Yiddish Poet and His Translator," *Yiddish,* Winter/Spring, 1976, pp. 70–71.

16. Eisland, *Shriften,* p. 17.

17. J. Luria, ed. *Dos yidishe folk* (Vilna, 1906).

18. Dubrovsky, *Yiddish,* p. 74.

19. *Ibid.*

20. Aaron Glants-Leyeles, "Schvarts, der amerikaner," *Zukunft* (December, 1961) p. 469.

21. Mukdani, "Y. Y. Schvarts."

22. Jones, "I. J. Schwartz in Lexington," p. 28. Jones presents an extended discussion of how the poet uses a local setting and elements of local history to demonstrate a new society emerging out of the mixture of various cultures.

23. Dubrovsky, *Yiddish,* p. 72.

24. James I. Miller. *A Critical Guide to Leaves of Grass.* (Chicago: The University of Chicago Press, 1970) p. 230.

25. *Zukunft* (August, 1921) p. 520.

26. William Faulkner is generally credited for his sympathetic treatment of blacks. His first book, *Soldiers Pay,* was published in 1925, three years after *Kentucky* was completed.

27. Jones, "I. J. Schwartz in Lexington," p. 28.

28. Leo Dinnerstein, *The Leo Frank Case* (New York: Columbia University Press, 1968). The ex-populist and racist politician Tom Watson launched this hate campaign. The case aroused the Jewish community world wide, and enlisted the support of prominent Jews and Gentiles across the nation. The Yiddish press followed the story closely and Schwartz was certainly aware of the case before moving to Kentucky.

29. Steven Hertzberg, *Strangers within the Gate City: The Jews of Atlanta 1845–1915* (Philadelphia: The Jewish Publication Society, 1978) p. 215.

30. See "Parting" in the Appendix for the promise Schwartz made to his own father.

31. Perry Miller, ed., *Major Writers of America,* Vol. 1 (New York: Harcourt, Brace & World, Inc, 1952) p. 1107.

Kentucky

To Mary and Tselia
With great love

I love the earth on which I tread,
 Fresh is the earth and fruitful and rich.
Virgin earth, so yielding, so mild,
She kisses and cools my steps with her grass.
The flavor of apples exudes from within,
The breezes fan and caress my cheek.
I know this earth is not sanctified by blood—
My father rests in peace somewhere else.
But my child belongs to this land,
Made radiant by its glow, made happy by its bounty.

Blue Grass

*T*he broad fields of Kentucky—
    Even now I feel the tender breezes;
The same sun casts its light on me,
And the trees shelter me.
And I, child of the wandering Jew,
Who first sensed God's world in Lithuania
With its lonesome forests
And blue, delightful rivers,
Found myself, on the threshold of my youth,
In the maelstrom of New York,
On the shore of the yellow Hudson
Where streams converge
From the whole wide world.
And I learned to love
The great, wild restlessness.
I was a spray from its waves,
A flash among lightning flashes,
Until the city became dear to me
With its victors and vanquished,
Its fortunes and misfortunes,
Its wealth and poverty,
Its surpressed groans and gaiety.
I love the ruddy autumn,
Parks poured from copper and bronze,
And the warm-blue sky.
I love the sea shore of New Jersey

Where the waves pound forever,
Spilling over from green
Into light blue and dark blue,
Edged with white lace.
Now, as my hair starts to gray,
I stand here in Kentucky
Seeing the soft blue sky
And broad, unbounded expanse.
Fresh, bright mornings,
Green tobacco fields,
And meadows of blue-green grass.
In the night, with stars close overhead,
Sounds reach me, here on my porch:
Horses whinnying, and
The soft tender rhythm of mandolins
Which are interrupted
By the resounding laughter of black children.

New Earth

One

A. After the Civil War

*W*ide, open, free lay the land,
    Extending to far horizons.
The sandy red tract stretches
Far and strange and lonely,
Bordered by low wild plants
And unknown herbs
With broad leaves. Free stretches of land
Not yet turned by the plow,
Untended thick succulent grass,
And humid woods here and there,
One tree grows into the next,
And root entwines with root.
From all this throbs, hot and strange,
An unknown tropical essence,
Of blossoming and decay.
Overhead, arched the sky, undulating and pink,
The evening sky of the south.
The whole landscape appears
Illuminated, bound
By red trees and rose colored plains.
From the blue eastern horizon,
Facing the burning west,
Across the red tract, the wanderer
Came with the pack on his shoulders.

Tramp, tramp, tramp, tramp, in the soft red sand.
Baked in flour-white dust
The tall bony figure bent
From head to foot—from the old bowler hat
To the hard, dried up boots.
The red, pointed beard bleached by the sun,
The eyes strained and bloodshot,
A world of worry in their red depths.
Tramp, tramp, tramp, tramp, in the soft red sand.

So came the Jew from afar into the unfamiliar,
His feet sore, his heart heavy,
A pack on his back, a stick in his hand,
Into the new, the free and enormous land.

The night set in—blue, wondrous.
At first colors merged,
Violet with blue and red.
Finally, one color engulfed the world:
A deep thick blue. Only in the west,
On distant black hills,
One dark red strip burned. And first stars,
Near and red, winked to one another.
With the onset of the Southern night
A great freshness arose:
The earth's luscious moisture
And warm odors
Filled the blue, cool air.
It was like water for the thirsty,
Like strong wine for the weary.

He kept going and going and going.
Suddenly at the bend in the road
The village appeared before him.
From the blue quiet darkness of the wood and field
Sound, song, and red fires
Burst forth suddenly, unexpectedly.
People spilled out from all the low huts,
Kith and kin, around the fires
In the middle of the street:
Clapping on brass and tin, and whistling,
Strumming on banjoes and singing,

Dancing strange wild dances,
Every muscle of half-naked bodies shaking.
Wild, in the red glow of the fires,
The black faces gleamed
With eyes red and heavy.
The fiery home brew
Went the hot rounds from mouth to mouth.
Heavy Negro women with red earrings,
Rolling and swaying, hoarse and hot,
Slapped themselves on their hips, laughing.
Naked children, with heads of black wool,
Jumped over fires
Like wild, young forest monkeys,
And kicked clouds of dust—
Up to the black and reddened sky.
Big black dogs barked,
And fat cats ran around in circles.

Through the reddish-black haze, the Jew
Passed with his heavy pack.
It seemed strangely familiar to him,
Known from old times:
As if he, himself, many years before,
Lived through the same.
So he went through the red dust.
Strange dogs barked,
Black children called,
Heavy women laughed,
And red eyes followed him—
Until the red wild camp was behind.
He was on the black field where
The old low farm houses stretched.
Letting down the pack from his shoulders,
He knocked on the nearest door.

From the house came a commotion.
The heavy bolt was loosened,
The door opened carefully,
And in the black void of the door
A tall, white, masculine figure
Appeared, with the black barrel of a gun
Extended in front of him, and a voice,

A hoarse sleepy voice, hissed:
"Who are you?"
"A Jew, who seeks a place to rest his head.
I am worn out and weary from my journey."
"How do you happen to be here?"
"I carry my business on my back. Night fell.
I am tired. My feet are sore. Let me in.
I'll give your wife a gift from my pack."
The barrel of the gun lowered,
The voice spoke out more softly: "Wait."
Then a figure in white came out,
A burning lantern in his hand.
Raising the light up to the Jew's eyes, he looked him over
From top to bottom and barked: "Come."
He led him into the barn,
Pointed out a pile of hay,
And said with feeling: "Don't smoke.
You may send the barn up in flames
Together with your pack and with the cows.
Take care." He slipped out of the barn.
And locked the door after him.

B. A Night of Dreams

*T*he stall was fragrant:
It smelled of dry warm hay
And the sweaty odor of horses and cows.
The cow sleepily chewed its cud,
And the horse snorted, switching its tail.
Crickets chirped into the night—
Long drawn out monotones—stopped,
Listened a moment to the stillness,
And again chirped into the night.
From far was heard another song,
The sleepy beat of a banjo.
A luminous late moon ascended,
And through the open windows near the roof
The moonlight settled into small white boxes;
Wherever a box of moonlight fell
Onto the hay where the Jew was lying,

Each stalk of hay shone in relief
And looked like a strip of silver.
Fresh breezes moved around,
Blew in the Jew's face and on his hands and feet.
As if his body were submerged
In fresh, cool waters,
His limbs relaxed,
Stretched out slumbering, oblivious,
And fell into a deep sleep.
The night stretched to eternity,
With pieces of broken suns,
With shreds of red, blue, and green stars
Floating in a chaotic sky
Of blue liquid.
From the bluish pale liquid
Thick greenish-red beams
Converged, forming
Rainbow rungs of a ladder
Whose top hung on nothing.
On the ladder were small black demons
With red, flashing, sharp eyes;
Up—down, up—down, they clambered.
Their bending, airy, thin limbs
Radiated from the black and blue liquid.
Reeling, turning quickly on the ladder,
Sticking out their long red tongues,
In a fit of loud wild screaming,
They badgered him and pulled his coat.
And then it dissipated.
A darkness settled on the world:
Thick, heavy, distinct, like black glass,
With red stars fitted into the blackness.
Suddenly out of the darkness
A forest appears,
A cold forest of gleaming guns
Advancing on him from every side
Blocking his path.
All his muscles strain,
The heart in his breast stops.
Suddenly, light and free and floating,
He lifts himself, swimming in the air.
His body dissolves—just a wave of his hand,

A movement of his foot, he swims, he swims,
And with his hand touches red stars
And pieces of pale cooled suns.
Through the long confusion of the night,
In the background of his weary mind,
His grief did not leave him for a moment,
His yearning homeward for his wife and child.
Every muscle craved sleep
As a thirsty man craves water.
Muted roars clamored to escape
From his constricted and anguished heart.
As a child complains to his father,
He complained to the Lord
Of all the worlds; he cried his heart out.
He recited Psalms with heart and soul,
With every bone, with his very marrow;
And he heard the melody,
The old solemn melody of Psalms.
Quietly, his tears flowed,
Escaping from tightly shut eyes.
Stubborn, fervent, the prayer struggled out,
The old prayer of Father Jacob
When he came to the alien land:
"Give us bread to eat, and a garment to put on,"
For him, for her, for his pale children.
As the blue morning approached,
And birds began to call,
His pained heart quieted.
He saw himself in a green field
Bathed in a tremendous light
It sprouts, it greens, it blossoms, it pours forth bread
With the powers of the first seven days.
And see! He has taken hold in the soil,
In the blackish, rich, wild earth.
He feels as if he drives roots into the earth.
And the roots suckle the earth.
A tree, an oak, spreads wide
Its fresh young branches, covered with green,
Soft, fragrant leaves.
Birds twittering and nesting.
Fresh breezes blow on him.
Over him hangs a cool round sun
Which strokes and caresses him with thin rays.

Greenish-blue in the morning light,
He remains quietly in the hay.
He opens his eyes wide,
His heart beating loud with excitement.
From his heart a song comes out,
A prayer to the Lord:
"God of Abraham,
Of Isaac and of Jacob,
Who hast led Your servant
Here, and will lead me further,
It is probably Your will and Your wish,
To plant me in the wilderness,
To make known Your name among the nations.
Do not hide Your face from Your servant,
Lead me through danger and suffering and darkness
As long ago You led
Your chosen people for all of forty years
To the wished for and promised land. Amen."

C. Morning

*T*he farmer* threw open the door of the barn
And into the cool stall burst
The reddish light of the rising sun.
Into the stranger's eyes flashed
The new, unfamiliar, fresh world:
Blue skies and thick grass,
Distant woods under a green leafy crown,
Nearby fruit trees covered with dew,
White-washed walls of the house
Bathed in green up to its windows.
Quietly the woman of the house approached
In a yellow straw hat with a wide brim;
From her open tanned face and gentle eyes
She glanced at him.
Wearing a white cotton house dress

---

*Schwartz uses the word *goy* which means a gentile or non-Jew. The word has acquired pejorative connotations in English and thus would not be appropriate to the meaning. My original translation for *goy* was "Christian," but Schwartz himself suggested that the word was too awkward and that I substitute "farmer."

She sat down to milk the cow.
The white frothy streams
Sang and danced as they squirted
Against the bottom of the shining pail.
The air smelled of warmth and abundance.
The farmer led him to the well;
And when the stranger washed
In the cold, clear water, the daughter
Approached him with a
Coarse white homespun towel.
The little ones, fingers in their mouths,
Their blond hair uncombed,
Timidly followed him with their blue eyes.
They shifted positions like geese on little brown legs,
Pinched one another, pushed each other,
Until the farmer chased them away
And invited the stranger to his table.
Thanking him, the Jew explained
That first he must pray, he must praise God.

He wrapped himself in his prayer shawl,
A large one with black stripes,
Put on the little four-cornered boxes
With hanging black straps.
Man and wife and child stood motionless,
Astonished and amazed. The strange man
Turned his face to the wall,
Closed his eyes, and with fervor
Rocked, rocked his bony body.
Afterwards he washed his hands again,
Intoned a short prayer—
And only then began to break his bread.
He didn't touch the meat.
He sat with his hat on,
And dipped black bread into the milk.
The farmer found his tongue.
He marveled at all the amazing things
Which he had seen for the first time.
He had, he said, traveled the world over
And had never seen and never heard such things.
The garment with the stripes he could understand,
But what are those boxes with the straps for?
And do all Jews pray exactly as he does?

36

At that the Jew smiled quietly.
A pious Jew, he explained, ought to do
As is written in the Old Testament,
As God commanded Moses, His servant.
The farmer, still marveling,
Insisted that he had never,
Until that day, heard of such things.
After the meal was over,
When the Jew closed his eyes
And again began to murmur quietly,
The farmer gave his wife a wink:
A pious man, he keeps on praying.

After the initial surprise had passed,
Everyone felt more at ease.
The farmer expansive, cheerful, lit
His short black pipe, and the Jew
Beginning to talk, unburdened himself.
He came, he said, from hell, from a city
Where people do not live, but fall under the yoke.
He suffered in that big, wild city.
He was a tailor fifteen hours a day,
Confined in a narrow hole
Without a drop of air, without a bit of sunshine.
His flesh started to shrivel
And every bone in his body sensed death.
His heart began to grieve
For himself, for the years of his youth.
And he, living, grieved
For his orphans
Whom he had not seen for years
While wandering in search of bread.
So, with a pack, he set out on the road.
Here, at least, he has the open sky,
The world is wide, and people good;
A Jew does not get lost, as they can see.
Quietly, sedately, the farmer kept on puffing,
Covering himself with curtains of smoke,
Putting a word in here and there,
While his wife wiped her eyes.

"That's all," said the stranger, "A Jew lives with trust."
He believes that God will not abandon him either.

And what does he desire: riches? money?
He wants only to reach the shore
And know that this is the place of refuge
God has destined for him. He is tired.
His every limb craves rest,
A roof of his own, a corner of his own.
He yearns to work in the sweat of his brow.
Does he look for more than a piece of bread?
He has wandered the length and breadth
Of the great new world. The land is rich,
It is fresh and young. The people are rough
But beneath their shells beat
Good hearts with compassion for strangers.
He saw how Jews,
Settling among Christian neighbors,
Engaged in selling products of the land.
They buy a skin, a bundle of wool, furs
Metals—plentiful here—they trade.
They work diligently and make a living.
The farmer sat quietly and thought,
Looked into the Jew's weary face,
Slowly stood up from his seat,
Knocked the gray ash from his pipe,
And patted him upon the back:
"Don't leave now, Jew.
I am going to meet with neighbors today;
We'll talk things over, then we'll see."
From the threshold the farmer called to his wife:
"Do not let the Jew budge from this place."

D. The End of the Pack

*A*s the day drew to a close
   And the slanted red rays fell,
The neighbors gathered.
Stout farmers arrived
With coarse calloused hands,
Ruddy faces and necks.
All wore baggy white pants,
Shirts unbuttoned, open on the chest,
Wide, straw hats on their heads.
The only one who was distinctive

Was the tall thin pastor
Dressed in black, every button
Fastened up to his neck. Behind the men
Came the quiet devout women
With thin drawn lips;
Reserved and hushed, only their eyes
Spoke eagerly and quickly,
Sliding from one face to the next.
They sat down on the porch,
The men separate and the women separate.
Immediately there rose,
From each man a puff of smoke.
(But no smoke came from the thin pastor.)
The hostess brought from the cellar
A heavy crock of cold apple cider
Bubbling up to the black rim.
She went around with eyes averted
Serving the smoking guests.

The Jew, stranger that he was, sat quietly.
Alien, he sat among the unfamiliar crowd.
Shyly, from the corner of his eyes, he looked
At the heavy bodies and necks,
As oaks rooted in the soil,
He felt helpless and weak
He sat forlorn, preoccupied,
His head down, his neck bent,
Not daring to raise his eyes.
Softly, the host started
To speak: "Neighbors"
"I told all of you about the Jew.
Here he sits, a stranger among us.
What can we do for him?" At this the pastor,
Quiet and sedate, spoke out:
"First, let's hear from the Jew,
And then we'll see." They agreed
And they all grunted "Right, right."
So the Jew told his story anew.
Above all else, they were touched by the sorrow
Crying out from his eyes,
By the frequent sigh which accompanied
The foreign pronunciation, the strange intonation
Of familiar words. The sorrow

Of the lonely, homeless man was
In every tone, in each unintelligible word.
And when the Jew stopped talking
Everyone sat quietly a while, their heads
Bent in the red evening light,
Heart talking mutely to heart.
Although they appeared hard as iron,
Their hearts still responded to suffering
For they, themselves, in early childhood,
Had known the taste of loneliness and sorrow.
They heard from fathers and from old grandfathers,
The first pioneers, of the life and death
Battle with the red man,
Of sleeping with a gun in hand for fear
Of sudden fires and tomahawks.
The sorrow of the lonely stranger
Touched the brave, silent hearts.

Now the thin pastor stood up,
Stroked his pale, high forehead,
And clearly, slowly, started to talk.
He began with the patriarchs:
With Abraham, Isaac, and Jacob,*
He told of Joseph in the alien country,
Of the prophet Moses with the Ten Commandments,
Of old King David with the Psalms,
Until he came to the son of God,
The lord, Jesus Christ. "Because of that,"
He concluded,
"Open your door to the stranger who knocks."

One of the neighbors began,
Old Tompkins, with the face of a lion,
Hair, brow, and beard gray:
"My old barn and the house by the pond
Are standing empty, neglected. Let the Jew
Move in there and do business.
I won't charge him any money for it.
Later, if he can, let him buy it.

---

*The Jew, in his night of dreams, also calls upon these patriarchs. Schwartz distinguishes the Jewish patriarchs by giving the Hebrew spelling of their names, while the names in the mouth of the Pastor are transliterated from the English into Yiddish.

I'll sell it cheap."
                    "Good, that's good,"
The host thanked him kindly.
"But what do we do about the old place
That is in danger of collapsing?
We'll kill our Jew yet,"
He quipped.
                    "I'll give lumber,
As much as is needed to fix up the house,"
The lumber merchant said.
"We'll fix the house and the barn,"
They spoke up from every corner.
"But we need money to carry on a business,"
The host persisted.
"If I sell the merchandise in my pack,
I'll have enough," put in the Jew.
"Fine, Fine, a good idea, no need for a better one.
Hey, mother, let's have the pack over here."
And in reply, the pack appeared at once
And was unpacked.
Onto the white world crept
Blue, red, pink, green
Knitted jackets for women,
Dresses of the most flaming silk,
Tablecloths with blue and red squares
And heavy, thick golden fringes,
Striped colored shirts for the men,
Pipes of golden amber,
And heavy silver watches like onions,
Long strings of glass beads
In gaudy rainbow colors,
White silvery pocket knives
With green tinged steel blades,
Sea-shells, mother-of-pearl, bone,
Green and pink playthings for the children,
All kinds of beads and eyeglasses.
And over this, as if suddenly on fire
A large, red, sun flamed.
The people squinted
And protected their eyes from the flames.
They looked at each other astonished,
Dazzled by the scream of colors.
Later they smiled into their whiskers.
Their wives continued to sit quietly,

Like geese, they craned their necks from afar,
Their eyes blazed.
"Hey, women, now it's your turn. Come
Show your stuff." So the women,
Sedate and quiet, came over,
At first with restrained movements,
But soon, as if they were at a fair,
They became more animated and cheerful,
Their eyes bright, as if on fire,
Their voices lively,
Their hands working deftly
As each one made a pile for herself.
The hostess was flushed,
Bustling, running among the customers,
Coming often over to the Jew
To ask the price of an article:
"Tell me only what the thing cost you,
And I'll set the price for them, myself."
The Jew sat ashamed
Among the smoking, joking men.

It got darker.
The excitement and merriment
Set with the sun.
The women, quiet once more,
Retired again to their corner.
The faces became earnest,
They got up, began to yawn,
And quietly prepared to leave,
The men led the way, smoking their pipes,
The women walked behind with their new linens.
The men slapped the Jew on the back:
"What is your name?"
                    "Joshua."
"Fine name.
From now on we'll call you Josh."
And they withdrew into the night.

E. In the New Land of Canaan

O n a fresh, clear, summer day
The loud banging of iron reverberated.

The spacious yard was full of scrap:
Pieces of old, rusty iron,
Thousands of dusty old bottles
Which sparkled silver and green
In the glare of the hot summer sun.
A dozen hens pecked in the yard,
And the aristocratic rooster with spurs
Proudly ordered them around.
The old barn was strewn
With rags, with paper, with horse bones.
The sharp smell of wet, bloody, salted
Hides assaulted the nose.
And a cloud of flies buzzed.
At the entrance to the yard, the old shack,
Propped up by slanting railroad ties,
Looked young with its sparkling windows,
And smoke blowing from its new chimney.
In the shadow of the old barn
Were two bent figures:
A big black man knelt,
Half naked, his body glistening, his red tongue
Clenched between his teeth.
He gripped a piece of iron in his hands;
The Jew hit the iron,
Swung the heavy hammer and banged,
And ever time the hammer fell
And struck the gray iron,
The Negro jumped back
Without taking his heavy red eyes
From the hammer flying in the air.
The Jew's face was tanned
His tapered bronze beard blackened
By dust. For all that, his eyes
Had acquired a new radiance.
His tall, pale, silent wife,
Wearing her dark wig,* often
Ran out of the house to look for
Little Yankele. Now he is perched
On the high pile of iron,

*Traditional Jewish women keep their heads covered. They usually wear scarves but on special occasions, a wig.

Not knowing how to climb down,
And now he takes a walk on the narrow beams
Of the high, old barn; he jumps into the wool
Turning somersaults. He could break his neck.
And often she finds him, of all places, on the neck
Of the tall, stout, glistening Negro.
He sits on the Negro's shoulders, and drives him on,
He kicks him with his small brown feet,
And jabbers in a strange tongue.
The Negro dances and runs around the yard,
And jumps, his black feet like iron,
On glass bottles and sharp metal.
The mother's heart sinks, she trembles,
Lest that wild black man, forgive the thought, should,
God forbid, hurt her child.
Her husband watches this scene
But remembering another time in the barn,
He stands and looks in wonder and amazement
And sees in everything the hand of God.

Two

A. New Life

A small tree stands on hard rocky ground.
The winds beat, breaking its branches,
A yellow sun burns mercilessly
And peels and splits its sick bark;
Here a piece has fallen off completely,
The place dries, scarred, and smarts.
It shrivels, turns brown, black,
And the few yellow leaves of the tree
Wither from the sun and tremble in the wind.
And yet, the roots keep digging deeper
And have a life and death struggle with the rock.
They stretch their thirsty mouths,
And burrow under dead stones
Through dry sands, seeking sustenance
Until they reach the watery ground.
And suddenly, behold: the sapling has become a tree.
The branches, like swollen veins,
Are dark; they've turned blackish green,
Fresh shoots sprout from
Thin withered branches.
Now the bark is smooth, supple, shiny,
Fresh and moist. And the leaves
Multiply, and turn dark green.
They become thick and heavy.

You watch and a shadow appears on the earth,
Green strips of grass appear on the yellow sand,
Green branches sway in the yellow heat,
And the green is alive with the sound of birds.

The old house has come to life again,
With new people from an old tribe:
The small window-panes have begun to sparkle,
And on the door frames shine
White tin *Mezuzah*. Inside, on a crooked wall,
Cool and freshened with whitewash,
Hangs a red and green *mizrekh*
Embroidered with shining silken thread—
A distant memento from the bridal years.
Around the *mizrekh,* pictures of rabbis,
Of stern Jews with high foreheads,
Black satin caftans, fur brimmed hats,
Faces of transparent parchment,
With hooked noses and long beards.
And somewhat removed from them, the faces
Of virtuous mothers, great-grandmothers,
With soft eyes and tightly drawn lips,
With fancy kerchiefs on their heads
And pale pearls on pale necks.
Whenever the crooked wall shakes
From the banging of the iron outside,
The mothers bounce away from the wall
Looking at each other in surprise.
In the corner, on the whitewashed shelf,
Together with the brass Sabbath candlesticks,
The old holy books brought from home*
Stand sleepily absorbed in themselves.
Old *Reb Bekhaye* in yellow bindings,
The set of *Mishna* and the leather-bound *Eyn yankev,*†
With pointed letters from the Amsterdam press:
And close by, nestled lovingly,
Is the tear-stained women's Bible

---

*The European birthplace was called "home" by many immigrants.

†The text reads *vayberisher taytsh-khumesh* which literally means a women's *Pentateuch*. This is a Yiddish version of the first five books of the Old Testament, traditionally read mostly by women who have not studied Hebrew as men have.

With pointed, crooked letters,
And black decorations on the white and yellowed text.
The house now smells of potatoes,
And the savory warm odor of chicken.
Through the window often wafts
The salty and bloody smell of a hide.
From a corner, from the old chest,
Comes the thin, pale smell
Of old silk from the mother's home, yellowed linens,
Heavy cool linen tablecloths
Which still carry from the old country
The rich smell of yellow citrons,
Green myrtle leaves from the *lulev** branch,
Bay leaves, and sweet black cloves
From the old and blackened spice-box.†

For six days there is banging in the yard
From early morning until late at night.
A hint of day, and he is gone from the house.
Wagons arrive, whips snap,
Donkeys stamp stubbornly, horses snort
The tumult is continuous:
The weighing, measuring, haggling over weight,
Arguing, jangling of money.
It is like a thick dust.
There is barely time during the hot lunch hour
To grab a bite of potatoes and sour milk.
He keeps one eye on the yard, where the chickens scratch,
And the Negro lies stretched out in the sun
Covered with a swarm of bloodthirsty flies.
The woman is in harness all day long
Silently trudging in the yoke:
Little Pearl, weak and pale,
Sits in the sun, quiet, preoccupied,
Her big eyes see everything

---

*Schwartz makes reference here to a traditional ceremony which takes place during the *Sukkoth* holiday. A palm branch and a citron, symbols of the festival, are carried and waved in the synagogue and benedictions are said over them. Traditional homes have a *lulev* (palm branch) and *esrog* (citron) for *Sukkoth*.

†A perforated container to hold spices used in the *havdalah* ceremony, the ceremony performed at the close of Sabbath to distinguish between its holiness and the profaneness of the ensuing weekdays.

And see nothing; she dreams.
If you don't remind her, she will forget about eating.
The little boy is a devil, he must be watched:
He jumps on wagons, climbs on the donkeys,
Mocks and imitates white and black.
The farmers chase him with whips,
Now the woman of the house comes running
And saves him from Esau's hands.*
She takes care of the chickens and the cow,
And if she has a free moment,
She washes, irons, and mends.
And when her husband comes home at nightfall,
He falls asleep right after eating,
His weary head dumb on the table.
Thus the whole hard week races by
Until beloved Friday comes to the world.
As Friday starts to fade
And shadows grow tenuous and pink,
The banging of iron stops.
The last loud bang vibrates
In the cool blue air and dissipates.
The Black man slips lazily away,
The wide gate is locked,
And from the distant blue horizon
To the nearest water of the river
The deep blue air of holy Sabbath†
Settles over the alien world.
The house begins to feel like the old home:‡
The children are scrubbed, their hair washed,
The crude table assumes a holiday face:
The ironed tablecloth sparkles,
While from under a stitched scarf,
One side of the browned, braided *hallahs*
Peeks out modestly.
The candles, blessed, proudly gleam
Reflecting in the grandmother's kind eyes.
The women's beloved Bible lies

---

*"Esau's hands," a common designation for Gentiles. (See Genesis 25: 24–27.)
†*Shabes Koydesh* which begins on Friday evening.
‡In Yiddish, the words *in der heym* (at home) convey often the home left in the old country.

Spread open to show the treasured decorations.
The odor of the spicy fish,
Peppered and salted, fills the house.
The last coals still glowing in the stove
Make the black pots gray with ash.

When the sun rises on the day of rest
And the yard discloses its iron and bottles
To the pure and soft Sabbath light—
Then the Jew takes account of his world.
He looks around at his children,
And singing aloud the weekly portion*
A great pity seizes him for the child
Dying quietly in the house.
He pats her little head with his blackened hands.
His wife now has the leisure to rest—
She consults the fine print of her Yiddish prayer book.
The father studies God's word with his son,
And in a soft wistful sing-song, interprets
The text for the week. He is sad
To see how the child grows estranged.
He doesn't want to say the Benedictions, he forgets
The little bit of Hebrew which he brought with him.
His wife complains about the eternal "nine days."†
Without a bit of meat one dries up and shrivels.
It's painful to look at the baby.
What does she have to raise chickens for
When the eggs are coming out of her ears?
Who can call this a life?
A stone cast on a desert island—
We'll forget how to talk to people.
But when his glance falls on the yard outside
Where iron and bottles are multiplying in number
And the Sabbath breeze carries
The smell of hides and raw wool,
His courage and assurance and comfort return.
He appeases her with soft quiet words,
With his clumsy calloused hand

---

*The entire Old Testament, read by observant Jews over the course of the year, is divided into weekly portions for readings which are specified and arbitrary.
†Nine days in Hebrew month of *Ab* when traditional Jews do not eat meat.

He strokes her head with its stiff wig.
She blushes as in her youth.
Don't worry. With God's help, it'll be all right.

B. Jake

A young duckling pipped out of the egg
Barely can stand on its thin little legs,
But presently, somewhere,
It discovers an expanse of flowing blue.
Suddenly—splash—it jumps in the water.
The red membranes of the little stalk-feet
Spread apart, free; they paddle in the water,
The red bill on the white thin neck
Dives, gags on the freshness
Of God's blessed streaming gift.
Waves glide over the little body,
Rinsing, stroking, rocking it.
The little body swims with its wet feathers
And is carried by the gray-blue stream;
The little duck takes to water.
Just so did little Yankele
Take to, and engage with, the new earth.
And not so much the earth, as the air:
The new, fresh, contagious air.
His Yiddish tongue suddenly turned heavy,
Moving clumsily in his mouth,
As if it were full of pebbles.
His pale, thin, and pinched face
Tanned by the sun and the wind.
The arms and legs thin as whips
Filled out, hardened, bronzed.
And in his sad dark eyes
A young flame started to dance.

He moves like wild fire. No matter how long God's day,
It's still too short for him: the yard is his,
The river is his, the distant woods are his,
The black man in the yard is his.
He is seemingly quiet—but when the Negro
Moves toward the dark barn,
Suddenly, a white sheepskin jumps up

Dashing impetuously, dancing on top of him.
The Negro drops everything,
Eyes frozen with mock fear,
Hands jerked up to his wooly head.
Shrieking wildly
He scampers out into the bright yard on all fours,
And behind him a sheep runs bleating.
A farmer drives up with his merchandise
And sheds his overcoat
With the large, shining, bone buttons.
He bargains and argues, smokes and spits.
Carefully, distrustfully, he counts the money
For the first, the second, and the third time.
When, at last, with God's help, the figures match,
He takes his whip and is ready to go.
He puts on his coat again
And starts to fasten the buttons.
He talks cheerfully, and buttons, buttons,
And—what the devil is the matter today?
It won't button. He bends down,
Considers the garment with wonder and fear:
It seems as if it's his, yet not his. In place
Of the glistening bone buttons
Is desolation and a void— the flesh torn out.
A commotion starts in the yard,
They look for the boy: the Negro is convulsed
With laughter, and slaps his knees.
The father is worried and looks around,
The mother comes running, smelling danger,
The Gentile, in the coat with broken windows,
Runs after the crowd, snapping his whip in the air,
The chickens fly around in a frenzy.
The youngster secures himself at the top
Of the high pile of rusty iron
And does not allow anyone near him.
The Gentile stands below, waves one fist
And shakes the whip in his other.
His father commands the boy to give back the buttons,
His mother implores the child
Until, finally, the booty is returned.
It falls in shimmering disks
From the high pile of iron to the ground.
His mother brings a needle and thread,

The farmer standing with feet spread apart
Holds the whip tightly, in wait for the boy—
Until the coat is somehow put together.

When the boy started school
His Yiddish tongue stiffened completely.
He was too entranced by friends:
White, freckled, gentile boys,
Getting lost for whole days in the woods,
Wherever God put a swamp, a nest, a berry tree.
They played Indian with old guns,
Paddling canoes in the blue river,
Coloring their cheeks brown and red,
And, sticking turkey wings on their heads,
They're ready to scalp the enemy.
The Negro children spot them from afar,
And all the little black legs run.
Their eyes stare over fences,
A little wooly head bounces up
And jumps back quickly—a rubber ball.
The little ones, frightened, cling quietly
To their mothers' aprons. And heavy Negro women
Peer cautiously out of doors,
Lit pipes in their mouths,
Red kerchiefs on their heads—and they gape.
Clouds of dust arise, heavy steps tramp,
The resounding cry of battle grates,
Inspires and frightens.
                                And when the boy
Returns home after battle—
He is flushed, blackened, smeared and red.
And hungry—as Esau in his time.
He has no patience to cut the bread:
He tears chunks from the loaf and stuffs his mouth—
What good is it now to remind him to say the Benediction!*

Nonetheless he is sharp at learning:
Gentile studies fare better.
He knows, he understands, he absorbs.
His eyes light up and shine,

---

*Traditional Jews say a blessing before eating.

52

His little voice rings with the love and the flame
Of the broad prairie and of young America.
Somehow, the South takes root,
Now he even complains about the cold north,
And is not pleased with "Old Abe."
Why did he free the black slaves?
His father tries to argue,
He tells him stories from the Bible,*
About Noah with his sons: about Shem,
About Ham and Japeth, that Ham
Is not responsible for his black skin.
But Jakey keeps insisting:
A Nigger is a Nigger—and that's that.
His father, listening, can only shrug his shoulders,
And the mother keeps silent, hears and does not speak.

C. Neighbors

*T*he people were raw, strong, and hard
With the instincts of the bear and wolf
That still lived in the forests.
They had the speed and cunning of the red man
Whom their fathers overpowered
When they pitted their strength against him.
It was a young fresh world
With the same primary ebullient passions
Of giants right after creation,
When one force fought the other
And one power swallowed the other.
It fermented, boiled, foamed, brewed,
As a new barrel of fermenting wine—
If you move it carelessly, it bursts.
Just so the young fresh earth
Upon which they trod
Fermented, brewed with covered streams;
Should anyone drive a pole too deep—
Thick greenish streams
Of crude and smelly oil
Would shoot high up.

----

*In the original, *Khumesh* or the *Pentateuch*.

Hot, fearful, in turbulent hatred,
And savage, unpitying in a wrath
Quenched and extinguished
Only by the enemies' blood. There were
No plaintiffs and no judges: each one
Carried his court in his own hands:
When one infringed on another's rights,
Each man stood up to the other
With knife, gun, and fire.
Right or not—his brother and his friend
Immediately enlisted on his side;
Whole families, old and young, wives and children
Fought for generations,
The cause of the original battle
Long forgotten by the battlers:
Was it an old broken axle,
Or a girl, hotly desired by two,
Or because of a drunken word over a glass of whiskey
Or a dirty look in the tavern,
Or over a strip of boundary land.
Blood spilled hot and red,
And in the hot black Southern nights,
The sky often burned fire red,
And red murderous fear
Exposed a patch of black night.
Guns cracked thunderously,
And wildly excited horses galloped
With black riders on their sweating backs.
And Sundays, when they came to town
From miles and miles
To hear the word of God from pastors,
The broad market place in front of the church
Was transformed into a battlefield
Of big-boned, tanned men,
With iron hands, bronze faces,
With strong black, brown, or copper beards,
Fire in their angry eyes,
And hot colored bandanas around their necks,
Astride wild, whinnying horses.
The black barrels of their polished guns
Were fastened to their gleaming saddles.

At the beginning the Jew was a mystery:
It was hard to understand his ways,

His strange attire and speech.
His every movement made him alien
And conspicuous to unaccustomed eyes.
But when they were used to one another
And the initial distrust disappeared,
They began to talk.
Miraculously, the Jew understands everything,
Knows everything that goes on around him,
Has for each occasion a good-natured, appropriate saying,
At the same time, both foreign and familiar.
A man like all men, he works day and night,
Collects old iron, bone, and rags,
And he gives others a chance to earn.
Yet, it was puzzling to them:
Why does a man work on Sunday?
Once, on a fine lovely day,
The pastor arrived in the yard smiling,
His hands folded on his backside,
Said a friendly word to the Jew, asked
About his business, patted the children on the head,
Bowed to the quiet woman.
A little later there arrived
Two or three neighbors; they sat down,
Lit up black pipes, as usual,
And then the pastor spoke quietly,
With a melodious drawl, as if in church,
Showing his mastery of the Old Testament,
Mixing in passages from Luke and Paul,
And from the other Apostles,
And finished with a quiet question:
How does he come to work on the day of rest?
The Jew countered gracefully:
He is a Jew and observes the old faith,
As the Old Testament directs:
Six days a week you should do your work,
But the seventh, is the Sabbath,
You should rest and keep it holy,
You and your child, your ox, and your donkey.
At this the pastor was surprised,
Pityingly, he shook his head:
Does he not know that Jesus Christ, the Son,
Had abolished rest on Saturday:
And in its place appointed Sunday.
Now the Jew answered pitifully:

He is unlearned, unschooled,
And not equipped to engage in a dispute
With one so fortified with knowledge.
He only follows in the path of his fathers,
And does as they did.
This pleased the thin pastor very much,
He rose and shook his hand,
Bowed again to the woman,
And quietly withdrew.
The neighbors stood up,
Patted him on the back: "Well said."
The next day the Jew received
A heavy, thick, flexible book:*
The Old and the New Testament,
A gift from the thin pastor.

D. Dixie Land

*T*he powerful skilled hunters from the hills
    Began to appear in the yard
In high boots and short pelts.
These were youths—ruddy and robust,
With young curly beards and hair,
Broad-boned, strong and tall,
Tanned winter and summer
Except for deep, white, puckered scars
In the thick hair of their cheeks, or on their foreheads,
Their ears split in half and grown together.
They came with the first light frost,
When dead grass shines silvery,
And the sun hangs low
Half silver, half copper, half crooked,
In a milky-white sky.
Single file, man after man, silent,
Thick fur hats on their heads,
Sharp knives in their belts:
Their mouths breathe
Small white clouds in the brisk air;
Heavy, white, unpolished boots

---

*Seyfer, the word Schwartz uses, means a Jewish holy book. Its use is ironical.

Beat out a measured rhythm
On the hard ice
Like soldiers marching to battle,
To the beating of a drum and the rapid sounds of buckshot.
Bundles hung down from shoulders,
And golden-red fox skins
Heavy with soft hair,
Flashed in the fresh morning light.
Brown shining mink,
Blue-black rats and skunks
With small round glitter-glass eyes—
Still smelling of blood, of snow, of woods,
Intertwine, and mingle as if alive.
The colored tails dangling as if alive.

They all made themselves famous
In the difficult bloody Civil War
With their steady hands and sharp eyes.
They were close to celebrating a victory
Around the fortresses of Washington;
They bled in the march of the armies
When Lee started to withdraw;
Many lived through the destruction
Of New Orleans, Atlanta, and Columbia,
Which still smouldered in their hearts
As a fire smoulders under gray ashes.
They still remembered the Battle of Richmond,
And the gray head of the chivalrous Lee.
The crying of old gray-bearded veterans
Wearing battle-torn uniforms
Still echoed in their ears.
But young life stirred in their veins—
And when their work was finished
They gathered in a corner of the barn,
Where the old glowing stove
Sputtered with red crackling heat.
They draw from their boots flasks
Of strong, white, burning whiskey.
Their eyes flash and grow big,
They gauge their strength, wrestle.
Their long hair falls unruly,
The laughter sounds hot and thunderous,
They gossip about the neighbors:

Who beats his wife, and who slaps her husband,
And whose horse is good, and whose better,
And who took whose bride away,
Led her away from the church on the wedding night
With guns in hand, and what the groom
Intends to do about it; they joke
About the families of bride and groom; there is
Red merriment in the corner of the barn,
Which spreads to the far, cold wall,
Over heaps of salted hides,
Horse bones, and old rags.

Sometimes they recall the war:
They list the names of friends
Who died in their arms
In cold, wet holes.
They drink "*lekhayim*"* to their memory,
And force the Jew to take a sip;
Hearts are laid open,
Vehement, excited words pour out
With fire, with spice, with heart and soul.
How that tall thin Lincoln
With the unscrewed limbs, long arms
And pale drawn out face
In his tall, shining top hat,
Came unexpectedly, unanticipated,
Into Richmond on a fine day:
No bell resounded, no gun cracked,
But suddenly, like wild fire,
The tidings spread: It is he, it is he.
And town and street were flooded
By a wild sea
Of crying, laughing black faces.
Their eyes gleamed, white and flashing,
Hands stretched out to him.
Small children were held over heads;
And from the bosom of the black sea
The roar of Africa struggled out.
Tearing and pulling at their clothes,

---

*Schwartz puts the word in quotations in the text to point out the irony of the drunken Confederate soldiers making a toast "to life" to their dead compatriots.

58

They broke into a mad, fiery dance.
Turning, convulsing towards the earth,
They cry in wildest ecstasy:
"My Jesus!" "My Saviour!" "Hallelujah!"
The pale face of Abe
Distorted with pain and woe.

The brave hunters drink excitedly.
Their eyes bloodshot,
Their white scars shining,
And from hot bullnecked throats
A passionate song erupts
Of proud, bold, brave Dixie Land.
The song, loud and fervent,
Fills the dim old barn
And bounces off the blackened ceiling:
A zealous outcry hot with pride:
"Hooray, hooray, for Dixie, Hooray!"

Three

A. Winter

*T*hat year saw a winter
   Glittering with frost and heavy snows:
Alaska blew into the country,
And birds, victims of the dry piercing wind,
Fell onto the hard greenish-sparkling snow.
The rivers were ice-bound,
And blue-green squares of heavy ice
Were chopped from the wells
And melted in kettles for drinking.
The community was cut off,
As if with a white, flashing knife
From the surrounding world. The drifts of snow
Covered every road and path,
And all the train tracks.
Twilight played its game
In the cold, rose-colored evening.
The distant hills appeared
Locked in white woods.
Green blue shadows looked coldly
Down upon the valley and the small settlement
Frozen in ice to the midriff.
Thick rose-colored hats of snow on the roofs,
Straight, slender columns of gray smoke

Rising from the hats
To the deep star-studded sky.
Later, the Alaskan breath abated,
And another wind blew in.
The gray sky descended,
And when the smoke from the chimneys tried
To rise into the air, the eye
Could not distinguish the smoke
From the sky. As if from a fine sieve,
Something sifted continuously,
Day and night. Neither water, nor ice,
It made the snow heavy, and the ice dismal.
When the ice-rain stopped
A pale sun shone.
Each tree was covered with glass,
Each branch of the linden, the chestnut,
And the small evergreen
Was covered with thick glass.
And from under the frozen prism
The black-green parts of the branches
Looked out in fantastic patterns.
At the slightest wind
The long, heavy, glassy branches
Rang in the air.
Tree and sapling bent to the ground,
Roofs sagged under the burden
Of heavy, sparkling, ice-glass.
Work in the junkyard came to a halt,
Iron frozen in the ice
Smelled of rust
And its driving cold kept all away.
In the house the oven burned day and night
But the old house was cold and cheerless.
Thick heavy shields of ice
Appeared on the walls
Like infected blisters on a sick body.
In the pale light of day
They spread a dark gloom.
The gray bearded elders on the walls
Froze and grew paler,
The thin-lipped old grandmothers
Grimaced, blue from cold.

When the thaw began outdoors
Cloudy drops, slowly creeping,
Began dripping from the walls.

Little Pearl, skin and bones,
Lay sad and quiet
In the big bed, her feet stiff.
The quiet, bundled-up woman
Poured boiling water into bottles
To keep her baby warm.
Sometimes she sat by the stove
For hours on end,
Lost in thought,
Warming her thin bluish-red hands,
Looking into the fire,
And staring, staring, staring. Suddenly,
As if waking from a bad dream,
She spit into the flame three times
And began murmuring to herself.

Pearl was not destined
To rise from her mother's bed.
Her thin chest rasped like a saw,
And her little face flamed like tinder,
Her blue eyes burned hot,
With a flickering light,
Her blond hair looked
Like stalks on a scorched field.
Under the pale cold sheets
Her poor little fragile body
Burned, burned, burned
Like a quiet setting sun seems to burn under
White snow on a winter field.
When the light grew dim
As if covered by a glass shade,
And her limbs stretched,
Stiff and hard, to their full length,
The tired breast of the poor child
Gave its last gasp
Like the gasp of a bird before quiet sleep.
The heat was still coming from the bed,
Red heat in the gray morning light.

The father put on his best garment,
Washed his contorted face,
And slowly let himself out the door.
He came back later
With two or three old respected neighbors.
The little body had already been washed
And wrapped in white sheets.
Burning candles were at its head.
The mother stood silently,
In a fit of mute sorrow,
Clutching at her swollen belly,
Her whole body trembling.
Overnight, the little devil Jake
Became the old Yankele again,
The poor little boy from the small Jewish town,
His face pale, pinched, and drawn.
He recited the Psalms through choking tears.
His little voice trembled, shook
In a heart-breaking lament and prayer.
When the neighbors came
Into the stifling air of the house of death,
Heavy dread engulfed them.
Looking down threateningly
From the moist winter wall
Were the gray beards and strange stern eyes.
The silent, stiff, pain contorted body
And Jakey's small voice in the strange song
Caused great fear
Among the guests. The tall Jew
Suddenly became foreign and distant.
He was not at all the same man who dealt in scrap.
He was stern, like the pictures on the wall,
With fixed, dry, red eyes.
Unconsciously the neighbors' hands lifted
To make the sign of the cross.*

---

*Schwartz here emphasizes the distance between the alien Jewish immigrants and the
Christian farmers by using a Christian image to which his readers will react emotionally.
Although the sign of the cross is a typical Catholic ritual, it is not unusual for Southern
Baptists or Methodists to also cross themselves. (Interview, Pastor Richard Blackwell,
Fellowship Baptist Church, West Windsor, N.J.)

The Jew began to speak quietly,
In a voice hoarse with sorrow,
His pale lips scarcely moving,
His eyes pained and despairing.
His black chapped fingers
Pointed in the air and
Towards the corner where the pale child
Was lying, laid out on white benches.
The yellow light made a circle
Around the small head.
"My dead child lies before you. I look for a place
To bury my baby, my little one.
I am a stranger here among you.
May God help you as you have till now
Been of help to me in my need.
Show your mercy to my dead one, too.
Grant me a grave for my child."
And his words with their
Trembling sounds touched all hearts;
Someone wiped a fresh tear,
And another kept groping
In his tobacco pouch
With thick heavy fingers,
Searching, searching for what he could not find,
His eyes buried deep in the pouch.
For a while all was quiet and dead.
They heard the flickering of the death-candles,
The Jew with his hands spread in the air,
His head raised, his eyes red.
The neighbors, their white heads bare,
Bowed in the face of death.
And then the eldest of the neighbors
Stepped forward, stopped,
And in a quiet voice answered softly:
"The cemetery is open to you.
Choose a place there among the rows,
And dig a grave for your dead child."
The Jew bowed humbly,
His face expressed thankfulness,
And quietly, he spoke again:
"Yet, one last wish. Like draws to like.
When my last hour strikes
I would like my body to rest

Among my own, my flesh and blood;
Our faiths are different.
Yet, all are dust from the same dust,
And we all serve the same God.
And God will reward you for the favor.
I ask a separate piece of ground
To start my own cemetery;
And if I am destined to live
I will repay this enormous debt."
Tears streamed from his pained eyes,
Running into the creases of his lips,
Losing themselves in the deep hair of his beard.
After he had chopped the little grave
Through heavy ice and frozen earth
In a remote rise of the field,
The well of tears dried up.
His eyes took on
Again the dry, sharp lustre.
When he lowered the child
Into the yellow pit,
And the first hard clods
Fell on the white boards,
A frozen, muffled sound
In the cold white stillness,
Only then did his wife find a voice.
Bent over the grave, she shook
With every new shovel of dirt.
Her fountain of tears opened
And her frozen voice broke through,
Forcing itself tearfully into the grave.
She begged the child's forgiveness*
And struck herself on the chest.
The words poured from her heart,
"Run, my child, run,
And intercede in our behalf before the Holy Matriarchs.
Tell them of our hard bitter life,
And beg them to intercede for us:
That Yankele should grow up to be a good Jew,

---

*Traditional Jews ask that the dead forgive the living for any injustices they might have suffered while alive. They also implore the dead to intercede on their behalf. The plea is accompanied by a ritualistic striking of the chest over the heart.

That your father and your mother should
Not know sorrow and misfortune anymore."
The grave kept filling up,
It was filled to the white edge.
The alien field stretched
White and quiet, bedded in snow:
Small white hills here and there,
Glassy crosses for headstones,*
And fir trees that reflect
Coldness with their deep green and snow.
Over white hills and blue valleys,
Over green frozen lakes,
Near yet far, a winter sky
Hung quietly, trustfully.
A cold evening sun
Cast pink signs upon the snow
From blue strips between white clouds.

B. God Has Taken, God Has Given

*T*he cold let up. A blue
    Sunny-bright winter's end arrived
With cold nights, frosty mornings,
And white crackling ice.
Each day the sun was warmer,
Kinder, brighter, larger.
The blue of the sky deepened,
And birds began to sing
From every crack of the old black roof.
Fresh breezes began to blow,
Dispersing a new scent.
And the trees came alive suddenly,
The black branches
Throbbed and swelled,
Into greenish-black buds
Smelling of luscious bitterness
And the ground sprouted
Fine young green grass.

---

*Southern Baptists and Methodists, as well as Catholics, place crosses on graves. Schwartz described a Jewish section in the Lexington General Cemetery.

The frozen house began to warm up.
When the noonday sun beat down,
The logs dripped
Heavy, golden drops of sap
Whose seductive forest smell
Crept into the nose and throat.
The windows opened wide again.
In the yard, early spring sounds
Vibrated cheerfully in the air:
The loud sound of iron,
The noise of wheels cutting into the soft ground,
The whinnying of horses and loud laughter.
The cow softly mooed in the grass,
And the young, newborn calf
With moist, big bluish eyes
Played with its mother's pink udders,
Kicking its thin legs.
The cow glided her flabby neck
Over the rounded back
Of the nursing calf, and the calf
Danced and nuzzled with pleasure.

Early one morning
Something awakened Jake from sleep.
It was thus: in the sharp blue
Of daybreak,
Something new was in the air,
Thin, shrill, stubborn squeals
Kept on annoying his ears,
Tenacious, as an angry buzzing gnat.
Jake pulled the quilt over his head,
He twisted himself into a round ball.
And good riddance. But there was hardly time
To find sweet rest
Before the thin watery squealing crawled
Under the cover and the quilt,
Creeping into his ear, pestering him.
Jake, straining with all his might,
Remained quietly huddled under the covers,
His eyes opened wide under the quilt,
His ears on the alert, his body tense.
Clearly, it's not a cat, it's not a swallow,
But something different. Quietly, slowly, he

Pulled down the quilt from his head
And saw his mother lying pale in her bed.
Trembling on the pillow was a little,
Red, wrinkled, doll's head,
Wet hair pasted to its forehead,
The small face all mouth. And it screams,
A thin shrill, long cry.
Jake lay with bated breath,
Until he felt driven out of bed,
His white shirt hiked to the knee,
His face flushed, lightning in his eyes.
He stormed through the house,
Screaming the Indian battle cry
At the top of his lungs.
Like the Black in his father's yard,
He quivered with wild excitement,
Every young limb vibrating.
Jumping all over the place,
He broke into a wild dance.

His father hired a horse and wagon
From a neighbor, leaving in charge
An old black woman in a red knotted kerchief
And smoking a black burnt-out pipe.
He warned Jake to take care,
And set off for the far city.
For three days the house was quiet;
The black woman sat around
Puffing out gray smoke from the black pipe,
And did nothing else. But when Jake, the devil,
Appeared in the house with his hue and cry,
She'd shake off the dream-smoke
And run after him with brooms,
Old boots, irons, black pots—
Anything that came into her hands.
The mother in bed motioned with her hands,
While the child suckled and panted,
Screamed and slept. On the fourth day
The wagon came back into the yard.
The father arrived splattered
With gray dust from head to foot.
After him, barely alive, came creeping
A Jew on short legs, his belly round,

Dusty glasses on his mild eyes,
Thick shawls around his bearded neck,
And long black boxes in his arms.
They dragged sides of beef,
Dark lungs and livers, spleens,
Smelly ox intestines and thick oxen feet.
The black woman then got busy
Singeing the oxen feet over the fires,
Chopping the heavy bones into small pieces.
Soon the whole yard smelled
Of a true Sabbath eve fragrance.
Clouds of flies swarmed,
And, buzzing, settled down to sniff.

The beloved Sabbath came
And the house was filled with luscious odors.
When the household sat at the table,
They found it laden with all sorts of good things:
First, the chicken livers and giblets
Chopped with onions, chicken fat, and eggs,
Browned cinnamon cookies
And little glasses of good kimmel brandy,
Cold jellied calves feet,
Salted, peppered, and garlicked,
Soft yet firm, easily cut
Into greenish-white, transparent pieces,
Greasy browned potatoes
Swimming around in large circles of fat,
The *kugel,* weeping, sputtering,
The sectioned *kishka*
Crying greasy yellow tears.
After that came browned meat,
Over which the knife had no power
Because the meat peeled off into strips.
Fingers dipped it into sharp red horseradish.
The father was covered with sweat,
The guest was covered with sweat,
Jake was covered with sweat.
The grandfathers on the wall perspired,
The grandmothers haughtily pressed their lips:
A fine feast, a really fine feast.
And the woman smiled from the bed
As if it were a holiday.

Between one course and the next,
They sang Sabbath songs aloud;
The Sabbath guest joked with Jake,
And threw him such questions whose answers
Either Jakey had long forgotten,
Or he had never known. The thought came up
As to whether Jakey could be counted for the blessing*
Since he was not yet Bar Mitzvah.
It was settled: they would take a chance.
But when it came to the prayer
It was hard for the tongues to move.
Tired eyes closed,
Heads nodded. Satiated, sluggish, the men
Dozed off into a sweet helpless sleep.

For a few days the Jew went around
Making a mess in the yard.
Quiet, small, a pitiful sight,
Feeling the iron and smelling the wool
But unable to see a chick standing there.
He sharpens the broad knife on his stone,
Tests it on his thick white fingernail,
And walks very slowly into the yard.
By now, the Negro understands; he jumps,
Making a racket among the chickens.
Feather fly, fear settles,
But the *shoykhet* performs the task unhurriedly.
He cooly takes the chicken by the wings,
Bending back its head, exposing its neck,
Compassionately plucks two or three feathers,
And slash—a spurt of blood, then a thrust to the ground,
And the chicken thrashes around in the yard.
The bloody knife clenched in his teeth,
He is instantly ready for another.
That man will cut up all the chickens.
If it were not for his little brother and the circumcision,†
He, Jake, would even the score.

---

*Post-meal prayer. The Hebrew word Schwartz uses is *Mezumen* which means a company of three to nine men, for whom the form of the after meal Benediction is slightly different from that prescribed for fewer, or more.

†The circumcision is a religious ceremony for Jews signifying the Covenant between God and Abraham.

When the time for the circumcision arrived,
They took the child away
From the pale weeping mother's breast.
Fed and nursed, he was sleeping.
The child suddenly started
To scream and shriek
As if just burned by fire.
Jakey could no longer endure it,
And ran out of the house.
He wandered in the woods a day,
His heart grieved, without relief.
When he came back in the evening,
There was no trace of the *shoykhet*
Or of his long narrow boxes.
Jakey was relieved,
But he was not destined to be happy for long.
He saw the cow straying aimlessly,
Not chasing the flies with her tail,
Not eating the grass, or smelling the air,
But grumbling with a sad roar.
His little heart began to beat faster,
And, out-of-breath, he ran into the barn.
Without searching, he found
The red, glistening, hairy little hide,
Still smoking in its warm blood.

The man with the beard
And the pot belly left behind another remembrance:
The Negro learned from him
How to slaughter like a "Rabbi."
Instead of twisting off the head as before,
He first prepares for the job:
Taking the chicken by the wings,
Plucking feathers from its thin neck,
Then rolling up his eyes,
He cuts into the neck with a dull knife.

C. *Sholem Aleykhem*—A Jew

*W*ho knows from where and how
Destiny brought that character there.
The thin long nose was alert,
The wide nostrils, fluttering and quivering,

Stood guard, and inhaled
The least breeze. On his thin face
Long mustaches moved,
Pointed ends turned up.
They had a life of their own:
Now they sit contentedly saddled,
Now they ride on blue razored cheeks,
Now they climb into the ear
And whisper something so funny
He has to laugh. The eyes,
So cold and secretive,
Not gray, not blue, but lively and quick, laugh also.
Tanned. Behold God's wonder.
The cheap garment on his skinny torso,
Narrow trousers on his spindly legs,
The yellow laced square-toed shoes,
Look hardly worn, as if they had seen
Neither sun nor dust during their long journey.
He materialized among the scrap
Like a sudden snow.
Just then, "old Josh" was engrossed
In a fresh, strong, oxen hide
Which lay spread out under him
In its full length and breadth, a hairy carpet.
This had been a tremendous, healthy bull
With thick, heavy, silvery hair
Shading into green,
And frightening deeply curved horns
As sharp as spears at their tips.
On the strong thickly ringed tail
With its heavy bunches of whitish-yellowed hair
Black flies swarmed.
The hide, just barely taken from the white bull,
Still throbbed with veins and blood,
If one stared at it too long
It seemed as if the hide would come alive,
Switch its tail, buck with its horns,
And turn the barn topsy-turvy.
In the meantime, Josh walked on the hide.
With all his strength, he turned
The inside up; it glistened
With pink stripes of blood, and white stripes of snow,
Fresh fat not yet cooled.
He poured piles of coarse salt on the skin,

And the granules took on
A roguish red color.

The stranger remained standing at the door:
His nose fluttered and wrinkled.
The smells didn't please it.
The mustache caroused, blew,
Just as if it were chasing flies away.
And his cool sharp eye took in
The whole barn, lock, stock, and barrel:
The big bales of dusty rags,
The long coarse bags stuffed with wool,
The heaps of dry, yellowed bones,
The spread-out bloody skin,
And the engrossed, bent figure.
As the Jew was standing
With his head in the skin and his back to the door,
A foreign, yet familiar, voice
Assailed his ears:
"A fine skin." He straightened up,
Turned hastily towards the door,
And immediately stole a glance at the skin
As if he feared the evil eye.
The strange guest caught the look.
Immediately the mustache started its game
And crept to his ears.
Josh caught himself in time,
Picked up a rag from the ground,
Wiped the blood and salt from his hands
And, extending a smelly hand,
Came towards the slight German.*
And now the nostrils started in,
The mustache snorted, blew,
The mouth opened red and wide
And ten measures of speech poured out at once.

Words spilled out,
A mixture half German, half Yankee,
Peppered and spiced with the holy language.

---

*Schwartz uses the diminutive form of the noun, *daytchel,* pejoratively. Not only does the diminutive carry the implication of slight in size, but it reduces the stature of the man and betrays the attitude of the narrator.

It was hard to understand
How he had come to this particular place,
But one thing was clear: the German
Had come here to settle.
Most interesting and curious,
He already knew every neighbor,
He knew about everything and everyone around,
And split his sides laughing.
He knew the Jew's goods and prices,
As if it were his own business
Where nothing is secret or concealed.
Advice spilled out of him as from a barrel,
His mouth didn't stop for a minute.
When a gnat flew in from somewhere
He froze on the spot,
Stopped in the middle of a word,
His nose and mustache stock still,
His eyes on the alert.
Suddenly—smack—a slap of his hands,
The nose and mustache start to move,
They begin again with the same word
At which he had stopped an instant before.
Later, the German ate with the family.
A countryman is a countryman. But the woman
Was very bewildered by him:
A savage, he talks and talks.
He's not human, but mercury.
Better nothing than such a Jew.
A bum, his mouth is on wheels,
And he is shameless before God and man.
She thinks he wouldn't even be afraid
Of eating pork.
On the contrary, he'd say, "it's very good."
He doesn't like the scrap in the yard,
It is not to his taste. He likes, he says, business
Which does not assail the nose so,
And where one can see the cash
Every day. He has
Thought of another sort of business, a fine business.
The matter is simple: the Blacks
Will have to start buying pants,
Because the pants that he once
Received from his rich white master

Are all frayed and falling apart.
Furthermore, the landowners have an abundance
Of old pants, jackets and top hats.
He will buy these at a good price
And sell them at a good price.
"Why not?" He stuck his hands in his pockets
And jingled handfuls of silver.

Later, after the guest took his leave
The house was finally quiet.
In fact, their ears were relieved.
It was as if an annoying, loud drum
Had played for three hours by the clock,
Drumming loudly, madly, stubbornly
And suddenly the drum split.
The Jew was left worn out,
The woman spat three times,
And opened wide the door
As if she wanted to ventilate the house.

Four

A. The City

*T*he community started to grow
    And step by step turned into a city.
Structures of red brick
Rose on high.
Large gold lettered signs
Glittered on the main street,
And windows of thick polished glass
Sparkled with gold and silver,
Highly polished furniture, porcelain and glass,
Heavy velvet and thin silk.
The wooden courthouse disappeared,
And in its place proudly stood
A large solid three-storied building,
Of heavy gray stone blocks
With dozens of marble steps
Ascending to the height of justice.

On the building proudly fluttered
The stars and stripes.
The broad square around it was covered
With find green grass cut short,
Leggy young hydrangea bushes,
With large white, pink, and blue heads,
Bloomed throughout the summer.

Later the main street was covered
With smooth gray asphalt.
The small frisky ponies
Harnessed to light, small baskets on two wheels
Pranced on short legs,
The dance beat of hooves
Echoed, cheerful and gay.
Silvery, shiny new rails
Stretched in long white stripes,
Joining the settlement to the city;
New red and yellow-colored cars
Squeaked and grated loudly,
Their shining little windows alive
With eager, unfamiliar faces.
On the broad, smooth market place
Arose, massive and heavy,
The proud knightly statue
Of brave Lee: the General sits
Gray, dusty, sedate.
And the horse remains frozen under him
On powerful dancing legs,
Muscles stiff, nostrils flared.
Lee sits and looks down on the market
From the high, gray, stony pedestal.
People and horses are like toys below him.
Multitudes of airy colored spots—
Purple, white, and blue pigeons—
Rise up circling above
The powerful proud horse-and-rider.

Half a city was still immersed
In stretches of sparse green woods.
Old oaks of giant proportion,
Wide and thick, still stood.
Here and there green kitchen gardens
Were neatly laid out in rows.
Fat, curly heads of cabbage,
Screaming red heads of poppies,
Tall, leafy corn,
Long, heavy, greenish-black watermelons.
Sweet peas in yellowed pods
Climbed on the fences.
A block or two from the dressed-up main street

Was a labyrinth
Of narrow, dirty, crowded little streets
With clapboard cottages like lanterns,
Without windows, without chimneys—only doors.
The cats dig up the dirt,
And naked children, black like the earth,
With round faces and red eyes,
Play with all kinds of dogs.
But the nights are festive:
Each house a shining lantern,
Fires lit on the street.
Poverty dresses in purple
And with a faint, seething laughter
Strums, tinkles, and dances.
Something distant and exotic blows in
From the hot swamp of a savage African forest.

Life drew one into the market:
On the old, silent, dreamy walls
Of proud Shelby's and Saint Clare's
And in their quiet stone cellars
Hung, rusted and neglected,
The chains and tongs of torture.
They shake in the air,
In the rude, alien, strong winds.
Old fathers with gray beards
Warmed their old age
Around young well-bred daughters
Who brought with them the scent
Of distant convents and finishing schools,
The fragrance of yellowed pages
And flowers pressed in albums.
The faint old scents,
Mixed with the reviving
New smell of young fresh blood,
And cool-glossy starch
From pressed white linen dresses.
In the dim white parlors they
Swayed over the piano,
Their fingers long, pink, quick;
Immersed themselves in the polished
Essays of Carlyle and Emerson;
Fantasized their tender white maidenhood

In the melodious poetry
Of young Keats and old Browning.
The sons were now strangers to them:
They had taken off their dress coats,
Cut off their curls and sideburns,
Discarded the knotted cravats,
And carried away by new, coarse fashions,
They went off to the raw world of business
Taking with them the coarse smells
Of oxen, oil, and tobacco leaves.

A grating whistle
Suddenly pierced the new pregnant air:
A noisy new mill
Joyfully blared out its message.
From high, smooth, white walls
Came a constant clatter, day and night,
And sounds of flat, heavy wagons
Loaded high with white heaps
Of rich plump fragrant wheat,
And ripe yellow corn.
They delivered, tested, weighed on the scale.
Horses and donkeys tangled,
And whitened Negroes bent,
Groaning beneath fragrant bags.
Inside the wheels banged,
And on the gray asphalt street
A film spread, white and thin,
Of fresh cool flour like white snow.
Three times during the day: in the early light
Of the morning, fresh with dew,
In the burning heat of the noon hour,
In the soft light of the glowing evening,
The sound of the sharp whistle
Spread over the city streets,
And dissipated on the far hills
Bordered by thick green woods.

B. Kin

*T*he yard expanded and grew.
Whatever scrap was available,

Whatever old rags and dead horses,
All found their way there.
The old scale groaned,
As people packed, weighed, loaded.
Heavy mules with wool hides
Moved as if lashed together.
The Jew trained new Negroes,
Breaking them into the heavy work.
From early till late wagons groaned and creaked,
Moving scrap in the yard.
The old wreck of a house was dressed
In smooth new fragrant boards.
Every spring, when the shining sun
Dries the damp earth of the yard,
The old door of the house opens
And out spills a spanking new creature
With new and curious eyes
And a loud squealing voice.
It gets in everyone's way,
Creeping, scrambling everywhere
Among the iron and the bones.
First they allow themselves to get stepped on,
And then they start to scream.

Later, kinsmen arrive,
Relatives from home
With shrewd heads and sharp eyes,
Fleshy, twitching noses,
Heavy bodies, good-natured bellies,
And jingling chains on vests.
These people had already traveled a world:
They had dragged themselves across Germany, Holland,
    Belgium,
Breathed the air of all the harbor cities,
Hamburg, Bremen, Amsterdam and Rotterdam,
Sailed the seas for months on end,
On well-known ships,
And, at the brink of life, faced the angel of death.
When the green turbulent sea
Yawned, opening white mouths,
Churning ship and sail in foam,
Then, along with the mice, they
Crept into a black, stifling hole

And recited aloud the long confession,
Tears in their blue eyes.
All this time, they were careful
Not to eat unkosher food, promised
To become good and pious toward people and God.
But as soon as their feet touched
The safe secure ground,
They mocked themselves
And joked about the journey.
Afterward, with their packs,
They measured Columbus's country step by step:
New England received them well,
Fed them potatoes and pork,
Let them sleep in the barns and stalls,
And bought toys for the children from them.
In Pennsylvania it was worse:
The fellow German was not at all happy.
As soon as he saw the nose and the pack,
Familiar from the old country,
He set watchdogs on them.
At last, they arrived— but barely—
In the sunny, far South,
At the home of a distant friend.
The smell of the boat followed them,
The smell of stale tar and rotting mice,
Mixed now with the smell of new barns.
But the eyes smiled free,
Bellies shook cheerfully,
And brass watch chains jingled
With every step of thick heavy feet.

They all spoke German now,
And drank beer in a big way,
Smoked thick, smelly cigars,
And delighted in themselves,
In a cheerful and well-disposed way.
Remembering something from the distant *kheder,*
They made the word *mazuma* famous.
After them came fat wives
With goiter-like folded chins
Big breasts and hefty hips,
Like round barrels on fat feet,
Wearing patterned Turkish shawls.

Their fat lips shone,
They chattered and gabbled like geese,
And believed strongly in eating.
They came for a week, or two,
To the Jew in the smelly scrap,
And filled the house with their fat.
No great pleasures for them there:
The Jew's room and board didn't please them.
A dryness reigned in the house.
They jabbered and shouted.
When at last the Germans went away,
The house at once seemed more spacious.

The Germans later dispersed
Over the length and breadth of the South:
One German however settled on the spot
And opened a pork butcher shop.
He stands in a white shiny apron,
White belly smeared with pink blood,
Eyes smiling guiltless and innocent,
He cuts the grainy pink pork
With a shiny, broad sharp knife.
On the main street, another opened
A small business with all kinds of linen
In clean pretty boxes on shelves
On which no speck of dust is allowed.
The storekeeper polished his window,
Painted his floor a bright color
And went around with a clean rag
Dusting shelves and boxes.
Or he stood, smiling in the doorway,
Hair parted and a pencil in his ear,
He greeted the passers by with a good-morning.
A third carried on a business in the hills
Near the cold black coal mines
Where Poles,
Thin Italians, and Slovaks worked.
Delivering all sorts of merchandise on installment
To the distant hick towns,
The Germans spread out.

Meanwhile, as year followed year
And the city grew higher and wider,

The old yard quietly grew.
The little children got taller,
Black heads and blond heads
Among the iron, horse bones, and rags.
They went to school
And brought home a new language
With new songs and new melodies.
The quiet woman wore out
Her strength doing the work.
The Jew, like the mule, worked hard,
Not knowing day or night.
The Sabbath was too short to sleep.
The old Holy books became, through time,
Old fashioned and covered with mold.
And *Reb Bakhaye* in the yellow binding,
Lonely and ashamed, nestled
Against the old forgotten set of *Mishna*.

C. Litvaks*

*T*he last to show up were
The lively, dynamic Litvaks,
Underfed, undernourished, faces green,
Bellies sunken like greyhounds,
Eyes sad and hungry.
They spoke only with hands and eyes.
With them they brought small sewing machines,
Milliners' frames and blocks,
Shoemakers' round, hollowed benches.
Awls and hammers.
This society of craftsmen from the old country,
Settled near the canals,
On Vine Street, Water Street, Clay Street—
The streets which cut across
The gleaming train tracks,
And where convivial blacks congregate
For a glass of beer and whiskey.
The Litvaks settled in shacks
With small, dusty, broken windows.

*Jews from Lithuania are called Litvaks. Non-Jews are Lithuanians.

The tailor hung out
A pair of patched, pressed pants
Which puffed up in the wind
And slapped passersby in the face.
The shoemaker threw into the window
A heap of twisted, crooked shoes,
Moved his bench to the window,
His shoulders higher than his head,
And with much diligence and zeal,
Banged nails into old boots.
The hatmaker put into his window
The round block—on whose top,
Pressed and festive, rested
An old hat, spanking new.
They settled in the holes. That was that.
Eating in the thick dust,
Drinking in the thick dust,
Sleeping in the thick dust,
They collected their pennies and saved
For ship tickets to send for wives and children.

Down from the old country poured
Green, thin, undernourished wives,
Thick blue veins on their coarse hands,
Eyes glittering like wolverines,
And with them, little children like green peas,
One smaller than the other,
Their ears and noses running—a proper entourage.
They arrived at the husband's business
With large packs of old bedding,
Two brass candlesticks, pudding-pans,
Bulging yellow samovars.
They unpacked the big, heavy bags,
Set up two or three small old beds,
Closed off the back of the shop
With red and green partitions—
And enough. They were finished with setting up house.
Mornings, when the children awoke,
The shouting started,
And the pinching, hair pulling,
Punching and scratching.
The mother jumps into the midst of the living heap
Of wounded bleeding devils.

Her small blue mouth becomes unhinged.
She thunders curses,
And before she knows it—aha—the husband.
Now she takes him to task
Together with Columbus,
And puts them both through the wringer.
The merchant of old pants stands,
Scratches the nape of his neck and gapes:
A sharp tongue, she forgets nothing.

Later, the trades mixed:
The bootmaker took in pants,
The pants-stitcher took in boots,
The hatmaker modeled himself after both
And, after thinking it over a short while,
Took in both pants and boots.
And now, the others, with justice
Piled windows full
Of stale smelling, crumpled hats.
Then everyone got angry and made sour faces,
Standing in the doorways of their shops.
With faces of fighting cocks,
They waited to greet the black.
The women also took a hand in the matter
And boldly goaded their valiant husbands on.
God knows where, when, and how
They learned of each other's lineage,
On the father's side, the mother's side, and the in-laws,
To the furthest removed generation.
They ennumerated the entire pedigree
And even crept into the other's insides,
Relishing it, seasoning it with melody, with song,
With white foam on thin blue lips.
But when a celebration came,
When one of the battling women
Delivered a baby, or, God forbid, a sorrow occurred,
They stood by one another,
Inseparable and sweet,
Balm for an aching wound.
They took care of the new mother,
Fussed, baked and served,
Cooked pungent soups,
And tended the children like lords.

Meanwhile, in the city,
A thin creature with a protruding Adam's apple,
Went around in a shiny long coat smeared
With blood of fowl and drops of fat.
His task was to go
To all the small stores with a prayer book
To drone and drum into the heads
Of the Maxies, the Hymies, the Sammies,
The accented rhythm of the weekly prayer.*
The blacks greatly enjoyed,
Trying to imitate the fine melody.
In addition, every Friday morning, he presented himself
At the break of day to slaughter the fowl,
And greet the fat women with
A hearty good morning.
At sundown, the women blessed the candles,
The men said the *kidush* out loud
Over the two home-baked *hallahs.*
The wives became God-fearing and quiet
And looked with respect at their husbands.
And early Saturday the men arose,
Duly put on the *tallith,*
Rushed through the Sabbath prayers,
Snatched a bit of cold food,
Pulled up the window shade,
Opened the door wide onto the street,
And were ready. The shop was open for business.

Actually, it was to be expected:
A person preparing for America in his small town
Learned that in Columbus's country
It's not a sin to work on the Sabbath.
The Sabbath before he said good-bye
He was called to the *Torah,*
But he, as well as the whole Sabbath congregation,
Knew very well: A month or two from today,
There, in the new distant world, he would
Be dragging himself around someplace with a pack,
Or basting trousers in a factory,

---

*A different part of the Torah is read each week. There is a specific chant to accompany the reading.

86

Or doing something that would be
against *Shabos*-law. The joke was
That one worked on the Sabbath
Even harder than on the weekday,
Because on Saturday people got their wages.
They fitted shoes and pants on Negroes,
And talked their hearts out.
But as soon as the stars appeared,
The merchant immediately stopped his business,
Withdrew quickly behind the partition
And said the *havdalah* out loud.

In any case, an eleventh commandment
Became engraved within them, which they accepted
And observed in its entirety as a Holy sanction.
The new commandment: "Thou shalt help thyself."
If they brought a brother from the old country,
He later repaid the money weekly
And thirty years afterwards did not forget.
They put the brother to sleep on the work bench,
And the next day escorted him out with a pack.
"Suffer also like us, and get thin and swollen."
They figured to the halfpenny,
And if one wife borrowed from another
A measure of salt, or flour, or a piece of sugar,
And forget to return it on time,
Then they had something to remember.
At the first open quarrel
They screamed about it for all to hear.
And this also was to be expected.
A person who drags a heavy pack on himself,
His feet swelling like blocks,
Dealing with dogs and angry Gentiles,
Or someone who is confined in dust
From early dawn until late at night
Banging nails in old soles,
Such a man knows what a penny means.
Monday at dawn, when a man and his pack
Marched off into the country,
He told his wife
That he would observe the Sabbath in the village.
But sometimes on Friday night,
After the candles had been blessed,

He would fall into the house.
Then the wife changed colors.
Not having expected him on the Sabbath.
He comforts her gently:
"It's all right, quiet, it'll work out somehow,
Add another dipper of water to the soup."

Thus, shriveled, pale Lithuania
Moved in and spread out
In the rich and blessed South.

D. Again Litvaks

*T*he trees bent under the burden of cool shining
    red apples
And transparent pink apricots.
The forest was still a forest: braided,
Branched, knotted, clustered, twisted.
And the density smelled of decay,
With wet mushrooms, wild raspberry bushes,
Centuries-old layers of wood growth,
Where one plant choked another
And grew out of the other's belly.
In the sharp bright moonlight
Lines of deer
With forest-like, thick branched horns
Still filed to the silvery waters.
Caravans of strong wild turkeys
Their powerful wings spotted with color,
And gray legs hard as stone,
Fled into the forest to observe the night,
Settled themselves in strong black branches,
And, at the least rustle, gobbled in their sleep.
At noon-hour, the air was full
With the smell of rich, heavy,
Liquid honey, like pure gold,
And the buzzing of fat, golden bees.
The distant plain still retained
The virgin fertility of young earth
Which ejaculated and implanted seed.
The grass was rich and heavy and sprouting,
And herds of fat oxen with enormous

Broad backs and horns moved around.
Cows dragged their heavy
Filled udders of milk in the rich grass.
Innumerable flocks of white sheep,
Like white mobile spots,
Rolled in the living green,
Like white waves in a green sea.
The farmer brought his rich surplus
From field and garden into the city:
Blood-red juicy beets,
Heavy white potatoes like stones,
Green and tightly curled heads of cabbage,
He didn't measure the produce by the bushel,
But distributed it in bags for small change.
A fat hen was sold in quarters,
And roosters were added to the bargain.

Lithuania fell into this plenty,
In the land which flowed with milk and honey.
When she learned how to eat,
She sat down in the dust of the stores
And started sending regards
To the languishing, hungry little towns.
The letters told how well off they were:
There is meat to spare, even in the middle of the week,
And what meat at that: chickens, geese, and ducks.
They eat bread made of fine wheat flour.
Large red, sweet watermelons,
Which spurt honey-sweet juice,
Are lying around in the street.
The skinny, shriveled relatives
Who fed on black bread
And watery potatoes in the skins,
Hungrily started to dream
Of distant seas and of the rich land,
From which came pretty pictures
Of daughters with smooth faces and sons
Dressed up in shining top hats,
Thick, heavy chains on their stomachs.
And with round grandchildren, like bulldogs.
But when the thin greenhorn woman
Had stuffed the bulldogs
Of the pretty pictures to the gills

With chunks of bread and honey,
She began longing for herring.
She took it out on her husband
And gave Columbus a piece of her mind:
His bread is no bread, his meat is no meat,
Here, a chicken is not a chicken, and, for that matter,
A brother is not a brother—and that's it.

The husbands, meanwhile,
Conscientiously carried on their business:
They trudged over road and route
With heavy backbreaking packs.
The man on the road made do with bread,
With a baked potato, with an egg,
Which the farmer granted him.
They slaved day and night in the store,
Roasting by the burning iron,
Clattering on the old sewing machine,
Talking their hearts out to the black.
And it was remarkable: how soon
The people without a common language understood—
Or more clearly stated—smelled, felt,
The naked nature of the strange,
Exotic and distant race. They recognized
Every twist, move, and nuance,
The sincere innocent laughter
And the newly acquired sadness.
They felt the spirit, and the rich tropic flavor.
It was natural that the black,
On his side, also immediately sensed that these
People were somehow closer to him,
Belonging, indeed, to the white race,
But a white race of another kind.

The German brothers turned up their noses
At the skinny Jews
And called them "green beggars,"
Making fun of their customs.
Just twice a year, in the awesome days
Of *Rosh Hashana* and *Yom Kippur,* the abyss,
The brotherly abyss, closed.
They came together to pray in a *minyen.*
After that they wished each other a good year

And parted until the next year.
The only one who, in a way,
Breached that gap was
The tall thin "*shokhet*"* with his knife.
But in the cemetery encircled by alien crosses
When a thin, sickly Lithuanian or German child
Could no longer endure the dust
Of his parent's business
And pined away into a better world,
They were laid like brothers together
In the small graves of the Jewish cemetery.
Because the first to be initiated into the cemetery
Were the wan frail children.
Small hills arose
With thin white boards for headstones,
And on the boards in the fine grass
The Southern sun revealed
The strange script—four cornered and new.

---

*Emphasizes a pronunciation by German Jews.

Five

A. Joshua

*W*hen Josh bought old Tompkins' place,
He felt, suddenly, as if he had
Taken root deep in the earth.
All at once, his eye grew more confident,
Cheerful, sure and contented.
His firm step in the big old yard
Sounded with assurance and strength;
His face was lively, chipper,
And in the creases of his nose and lips
A playful smile lurked.

For him, a chain
Of peaceful and industrious years began.
Steeped heart and soul in his business,
He did not notice how, through time,
He became rooted in the soil,
How everything became his own.
His English tongue acquired
Every nuance and expression of the neighbors;
He had a joke for everyone,
A friendly word, a short, clever parable,
Taken from the wisdom of the *Midrash,*
Which his friendly neighbors enjoyed.
If they had to build a hospital,

Or put up a new church, they
Came to Josh for a donation.
They listened to him.
And, in perplexity, they came
To old Josh asking for advice.
If the neighbors quarreled,
Josh often helped them compromise
And make peace.
Like new best friends, they then
Wet the peace with a drink,
And were surprised at themselves:
Why in the world did they need to argue?
The matter was so clear and simple,
A child in the cradle could have understood it.
And when the cup ran over,
They cried and kissed each other enthusiastically.
"Ah, Josh, he wears a head on his shoulders."

But later, when Josh carted
Wagons of red bricks to his place,
And set out to build a warehouse for himself,
They stopped
Slapping him on the back.
A thick foundation was laid
With large blocks of heavy gray stone.
After that, walls were erected
Line after line,
With even white rows of tall windows.
When the shiny red roof of heavy tin
Was finished at last,
It comfortably protected
The new, large, roomy building,
Four stories high, of generous length and breadth,
With heavy iron doors
On both sides of the length of the building,
And large lifts to carry up the merchandise,
Bright spacious cellars built
Of iron and concrete to store skins,
With presses and packing machines.
In a large bright office
A quiet kinsman already sat,
And wrote in thick books.

When this structure representing Josh's life was finished,
His head was already streaked
With iron-gray hair, and his face,
Was baked to a light brick-red.
Deep creases around a strong mouth
Smiled with hidden security.
The house and yard were full
Of graceful, strong, athletic sons,
And thin, Puritan daughters
In white dresses, and long braids,
With tan, chiseled features.
The old roots were now strange and distant
To them. Even he, the father,
Through time, had become estranged from everything,
Indifferent and cold to his faith.
If you give Satan just one finger,
He soon demands the whole hand; first
Josh missed one prayer, later, another,
And soon it was too hard,
So he stopped praying completely.
On Sabbath, he still closed the business
But without pleasure.
Instead of resting and looking into a holy book,
His head carried him to his business.
And the more the business grew,
The more the Sabbath became a burden.
Often, unexpectedly, on Sabbath,
He caught himself figuring with a pencil.*
For a while, he was ashamed of himself,
But soon was again deep in business.
The only one saddened by this
Was his thin tall wife.
She still prepared for Sabbath as before,
Blessed the Sabbath candles and said prayers,
And longed for the old times.
The radiance of the blessed candles
Could not drive away the workday atmosphere.
The heartfelt plea of the woman's prayer
Fell ashamed and superfluous
On the ears of indifferent foreign-born sons,

---

*Against the Sabbath laws.

And on aloof
Slender daughters with their foreign tongues,
Who read unintelligible, alien books
By the Sabbath lights.

At the same time, the name of the Jew
Sounded far and wide over the land:
From Kentucky, Tennessee, Ohio, and Indiana,
To Illinois and Kansas City on one side,
And to the furthest Northern states
On the other. Now they all
Traded and respected
The Jew's word, deed, and punctuality.
His word was a word: considered,
Dependable, and as severe to himself as to others.
His motto: "Mine is mine and yours is yours."
The business spread, branched out.
His volume and potential
Grew larger. It was
A wonderful, exciting game
In heavy thousands, in wits and nerves.
And Josh, the head, the achiever of this,
Stood quietly at the helm
And drove on to the wished-for goal.
Like all the strong and energetic
He did not like to stop and talk
Of the distant, lonely past.
When a neighbor who remembered him—
From that other time with the heavy pack—
Would sometimes say to him, "Josh, by God,
Some building that you built.
Ay, ay, heavy was the load
Which you brought into these parts . . ."
Josh mumbled something in answer
Until the Gentile, gabbing away,
Jumped to another topic.

They still lived in the old house,
Opposite the new, gaudy building.
It stood out because of its age.
The daughters were unhappy
But lacked the courage to speak out
In the presence of their father. But the mother

Was satisfied with the old house:
She loved every corner,
Every stone of the yard.
The old, crooked, propped walls
Were close to her heart.
Sometimes she recalled the dead child
Who was the sacrifice for all this.
And then, venomous and bitter,
She looked reproachfully at the yard
Where the four-storied building was rising,
Red, solid, and loud.
Although Josh, the head, leader, provider,
Seemed far removed,
Steeped heart and soul in business,
His sharp eye took in everything.
His intuition perceived
The needs and wishes of everyone.
From time to time, he said something
To one of his sons or daughters,
Which made them blush.
How does a father know that
Which has not been spoken.

He went around quietly now,
Disappearing from the yard for hours on end.
When he came back home at night,
A smile, which barely hid in his whiskers,
Played around his lips.
His gray youthful eyes
Followed the smoke
From his thick black, fragrant cigar
As it spread above young heads
Of daughters bent over sewing
And sons engrossed in books.
But cheerfully and significantly, he kept quiet.
He had secretly bought a home,
And was busy every day with the renovation:
Workers whitewashed, painted, papered;
The house smelled of new paint and paste,
And pine boards, fresh and smooth from the plane;
The hammer and saw banged
And the plane hummed.
From the windows of the remodeled house

Stretched fresh green fields,
Wide lawns and distant woods.
And on the fresh pine floor
Covered with warm sunlight,
Leaf shadows, jagged and pointed,
From thick heavy oaks
Danced in the gold and green.
It was hard for Josh to tear himself away
From the big secret which filled him
Like sweet intoxicating wine.
Often, looking at the wide field,
There came to his mind:
"Then God increased us,
And we spread out in the land."

B. Home

*W*hen Josh led the family into
    Their new spacious house,
They opened their eyes wide.
The new furniture sparkled:
Soft deep chairs of thick plush,
Shiny mahogony tables,
Tall, heavy, silvery mirrors,
An upright piano for the daughters,
And floors covered with soft carpets.
A dressed-up black woman was
Already at work in the kitchen,
Feeling at home and beaming with joy,
Her face shining,
Her eyes large and radiant,
Her teeth white and shimmering.
She was smiling from ear to ear.

The children stormed through the house,
Eyes flashing, faces flushed,
Up the smooth steps
Into the fresh sunny upstairs rooms,
With new iron beds painted white,
And small rocking chairs.
The house rang and sang
From top to bottom with young footsteps.

Cheerful sounds of young voices
Bounced off the white ceiling.
Then the turbulent young storm
Tore back down the stairs
To pour out its joy on the father
But stopped, silent.
The mother sat in the deep soft chair,
Her old gray head bowed,
Large tears streamed silently down,
And the father stood bent over her
Patting her head with consoling hands,
And talking quietly, as to a child.

Life proceeded in the house
With joy and certainty.
The young quickly grew accustomed
To the lordly new surroundings.
Their movements and their lively singing speech
Showed their new ease.
Mingled with this comfort was
The charm of the old, distant East
Which shone in their young eyes,
Something sad, yet ablaze.
In the long, cold, winter evenings,
The fire of red glowing coals
Crackled cheerfully in the fireplace
And seemed to twist itself
Into the soft blond and brown braids
As if kissed by flashing sparks;
The fire tossed flames on tanned cheeks
And was reflected in young eyes.
On quiet Sunday nights of rest
The piano beat out romances
And the front room was full:
Blond-haired, blue-eyed girl friends
And young lords carelessly dressed
In old-fashioned Southern costumes,
Hands, thin and white, nails pink,
Cravats, wide and artistic,
And hair in soft, large curls.
They sang in quiet voices
And recited old songs and ballads
With noble gestures and courtesy.

Then the lords bowed,
Invited the ladies to dance,
And young couples with flushed faces
Were enthusiastically carried away
By the rhythms of the soft, old dances.
Looking down from the walls were
Pictures of Southern generals
Made famous in the Civil War,
Wearing formal black coats and grayish uniforms.
They had long narrow faces,
Short, French-cut beards,
And feigned sternness in their eyes.
And from the library shone
The backs of the immortal Shakespeare, of Milton,
And Walter Scott's and Thackeray's novels,
Bound in gold and red, in black and white.
(The grandmothers and grandfathers of the old walls
Together with the old *Reb Bakhaye,*
Finally were laid to rest
Among the other old things,
Somewhere in a remote alcove,
In the neighborhood of the roof.)
                                    On free evenings
The house was always full.
Here people came to have a good time,
To chat over a pipe and red tea,
To ask advice about business,
Or even to get a bit of a loan.
Sometimes, the good-natured pastor came,
Now gray, with wrinkles on his face,
But more alert than ever,
Still loving discussions
And arguments about "the son and the father."
But now the Jew answers back,
Calm, free, cool, and smiling.
He lets the smoke of the fragrant cigar curl,
As he maneuvers very cleverly with the holy verses,
Which aggravates the pastor to death
Until he runs to the young to ease his heart.
The woman goes around dressed
In black silk, with pearls around her neck.
When they settled into the large new house,
Josh, her husband, took her by the hand,

By the red, work-worn calloused hand,
And said to her: "Mother, from today on
You won't do a thing,
You have a maid, you can tell her what to do."
Now, not allowed to work,
She doesn't know what to do with her hands.
They are superfluous and strange.
She can't find the words
To ask the black maid to do something.
She wonders at her young daughters
Who order the shining black woman
Around so easily and freely,
And at the maid who is happy to carry out their commands.
It seems as if the black monkey
Makes fun of her, and laughs behind her back,
And laughing, bares her teeth.
The poor thing, it was hard for her
To sit idle after a lifetime of work.
On a free day, at lunch time,
When the household was sitting around the table
And someone needed something while eating,
She hastily jumped up from her place
And made a movement as if to run.
Sometimes she caught herself in time,
Blushing and standing ashamed.
Often, her husband stopped her
With his steady hand:
"Wait, mother, the maid will bring it."

She sat through the long days,
The summer on the sunny veranda,
The winter by the burning fireplace,
Fretfully counting the stitches she knitted.
The ball of wool danced in her lap,
From right to left, and back again.
She shook "no" with her gray head.
She had enough to think about:
Her husband was somehow not the same,
Preoccupied day and night with the business.
Their sons, born here in this country,
Were strange to her, she cannot understand them.
Still worse, their young daughters,
Cold, proud, and conceited,

Were stranger yet than strange. Busy with themselves,
They were far from everything concerning *Yiddishkayt.*
What good can come of this?
The house if always full of young lords.
To the daughters, the old *Goy,* the pastor,
Is more important than their mother.
And wherever there is a *Goyish* celebration,
They are the first to arrive.
A tea-party in the church: they are getting ready,
They busy themselves baking cakes,
Preparing as if for a wedding.
And what will be the end of it. Do they ask for her opinion?
At this rate, the girls will become Christians.
And he, her husband, nothing bothers him,
It is not his concern. When she complains,
He shrugs it off with a smile:
"Well, what are you talking about: they are young children,
Later, they'll come to their senses."
While she is thinking, and knitting,
The socks and sweaters of thick,
Heavy, colored wool multiply—
Piling up in the chest, piece by piece.
It does not befit the ladies to wear
Their mother's warm and heavy socks.

But sometimes one of the children
Stopped beside her, paused awhile,
Kissed her old, gray head,
Talked with the sureness and tone
That an older person uses to a child.
He would pat her work-worn hands
Until her heart settled down.
That one was Jake.

C. Unity

*I*n the meantime, Lithuania began to merge with America,
Put a bit of flesh
On its thin pointed bones.
The narrow face filled out,
The eye became confident, brighter.
Litvaks still argued among themselves

But now with refinement.
They no longer thought
That a piece of bread was everything.
On free Sunday evenings,
When relatives gathered
Over a glass of tea and a cigarette,
Children in their arms, they said
That actually it was only right
To think about building a synagogue.
The children, getting bigger, were growing estranged
From Jewishness and the Jewish word.
The community, thank God, had grown,
But the Jews roamed around like gypsies
Every Friday night and Saturday morning
Looking each time for another place
Where they could pray together.
The talk about the synagogue was especially
Intense before those awesome days
When a man reflects on his purpose.
So they talked, talked, and put it off,
Forgot for a bit of time, and again
Started talking about it anew,
And again put it off for a time.

The discussion dragged on
Until Josh became involved.
The German brothers who were
At that time already on their feet
Could not bring themselves to join
The green, skinny beggars.
The German also started
Thinking of building—a temple—
But it was too soon to go it alone.
So Josh talked here, talked there,
Pulled strings in both camps,
Until he brought them together
At his house. The Germans
Put on airs in gloomy silence,
Smoked heavy round cigars,
And scowled. The lively Litvaks
At first felt lost
But later retaliated.

102

They rolled their own cigarettes,
And started talking slowly,
Solemnly, in half tones.
When they warmed up,
They talked with their hands excited and quick,
Until the Germans caught the spirit
And revived, as if out of a heavy lethargy.
When the tea was brought to the table,
They were all animated and at ease:
The Germans, with assurance,
Casually spoke a heavy English.
And the Litvaks countered:
Speaking quickly and freely, in German.
The German who cut the pink pork
Had a great deal to say,
And wanting to dig the beggars a little,
He called out: "Ja, but the synagogue,
It must be very massive, built of stone,
If not, the synagogue will float away
When it comes to—wait, how do you call it—
Ja, Ja, to the *Oleynu** . . ." That started
A big storm in the house;
The Litvaks became so outraged
They could have torn him apart like a herring.
The German was really frightened,
But then, the nimble Max jumped in:
"Yonder head," said he, "should not throb, because
This can, *javohl*, very easily get fixed,
When the prayer will come to *Oleynu*—
Then you must open your mouth."
He puffed up like a red turkey
And didn't talk anymore. Finally they quieted down,
And again approached the subject.
But immediately a second German got up,
Took the floor, and naively began

---

*The last prayer of the service before the mourner's *kaddish, Oleynu* contains imprecations against idolatry. Traditional Jews spit rather than mention idols in their prayers. The German Jews, who modified the prayer and abandoned the spitting, are mocking the passion of the Litvaks. For a discussion of the practice of spitting during *Oleynu*, see Max Weinreich, *Geshikhte fun der yidisher shprakh*, Vol. III, *Notes* (New York: Yivo Institute for Jewish Research, 1972) p. 231.

From Aleph: "Yet, but how is it possible,
A temple without an organ and a girl's choir."
Here the Litvaks completely
Lost their patience: they
Did not allow him to open his mouth again.
And this time, in a clear, fine Yiddish:
"Listen to him: organ—gorgan."
"Hey, who knows what that Austrian is jabbering about."
A smelly cloud of tobacco smoke
Hung over the whole house.
The Germans and Litvaks agrued, wrangled, screamed.
And people became hoarse.
Now the Germans felt very much insulted,
Indeed, they got up to go home.
And now the Litvaks were offended.
Josh worked hard to keep them together
And cleverly struck a balance between both sides.
It was late at night
When the storm was over,
The silent hostess
Brought something spicy and light to the table.
In front of the host lay
A long sheet of white paper,
And pen and ink were nearby.
The Germans and the Litvaks toasted *lekhayim*.
The red faces were sweating,
Wet hair pasted to the head,
And eyes were filmed
With clouds of sorrow and joy.
Glasses clinked softly
And a load dropped from their hearts.
Even the German of the pork store
Clinked with the nimble Max.
And when the crowd at last departed,
Josh sat for a long time at the table
His head bent over the large sheet
On which were written numbers and names.

D. The Synagogue

*S*tanding on a quiet street
Was an old church of red brick,

With long narrow windows of stained glass,
Which ended in an arch
Close to the cornice. A lawn
Of fine grass cut short,
And shady old trees,
Surrounded the church.
Thick, deeply carved ivy
With vines like young trees,
Climbed up to the coping
And filled the cavity of the windows.
Over the tall, narrow, arched doors
A plate of black marble
Was engraved with gold letters
In Gothic script: "You are Peter
And on this rock will I build my church."
It was cool inside
Like a cellar, even in the middle of summer.
The black polished
Benches extended, row after row,
To the high altar of the priest;
And in the deep, hollowed niche,
Lit by a red oil lamp,
Lonely and tortured, stood
The suffering figure of the pallid Jesus,
A crown of thorns piercing his head
And red drops of blood like beads.
On the right side of the wall, near that holiness
In the half darkness, were
The thick black undulating pipes of an organ.
Across the round smooth ceiling flew
Children and angels
With transparent shirts, pink wings,
And small yellow haloes around their heads.

The church dozed for long years
Engrossed in itself.
From eternity, it dreamt of eternity
Until the dinning noise of the screaming street
Reached it.
Businesses sprang up near the church,
Crowds of blacks milled around it,
An Irishman opened a tavern at the corner,
And nights became festive

With lively shouts and banjo tunes.
Later, small stores with displays
Of flapping pants and top hats appeared;
And then, a large lively chicken market,
Cropped up, noisy, tumultuous.
The nights screamed and crowed
With chickens from the whole country.
Geese and ganders gabbed angrily
And fat turkeys gobbled.
A shrewd Greek opened
A smelly restaurant; an Italian
Displayed the finest greens and fruit;
And Lee Hu-Tchung, with long stiff braids,
In a black blouse with tassels,
Installed himself in the white window
And day and night he stood with a small iron,
Pressing linens. Meanwhile, the church
Stood removed from everything,
Preoccupied with itself in the shadow of the trees.
Yet, every now and then, a sound
Separated itself from the tumultuous world,
Invaded the quiet nest,
Interrupting its thinking.
The elders
Of the church conferred once, and a second time,
Thought and thought, called together
The rich patrons to search out remedies.
But remedies, they could not find.
As it is written in the holy verses:
"Your destroyers and despoilers
Come from your own midst." Many
Of these patrons
Were themselves the owners
Of the noisy screaming trades
Which interfered with the quietness of the church,
But they could not help themselves:
Business is business, and church is church.
And now to the satisfaction of both,
Josh came along just in time.
He bought the church for a synagogue.

Of course, the synagogue had faults.
They stemmed from this: when

The church was built long ago
No one had anticipated that
It would be transformed into a synagogue.
Thus, it emerged with three faults:
The first: instead
Of the ark facing the east,
As is the law, it was placed
In the northern wall—but it couldn't be helped
Because the building was narrow and deep.
Second, there was no altar in the middle,
So that when someone went up to read the Torah
He had to go to the niche
From which the minister used to deliver his sermons.
And for *hakofes* one had to go around the benches.
The third fault was there was no
Separate place for the women.
That was the way of the Gentiles.

The synagogue was finally remodeled and
Covered from top to bottom
With fresh, fragrant whitewash.
The Father's Torah in its satin mantle
With a gold embroidered Star of David,
Nestled, solemnly and quietly,
In the niche of the recently departed Son.
And a large seven-branched Menorah
Of heavy brass with lions and stags
Stood by the Ark.
A quiet warmth and pious charm
Came from the remodeled synagogue.

It was the first night of Chanuka
When they celebrated the opening of the synagogue.
The small congregation of Jews, young and old,
The women with children in their arms,
Gathered for the celebration.
The synagogue sparkled,
Every lamp and every Menorah lit.
First, the people said the evening prayer.
The shadows of ecstatic worshippers
Swayed on the white walls.
When the cantor from the large city
Began to bless the Chanuka candles,

Accompanied by fresh, young children's voices,
The song reached the ceiling,
And solemnly bounced off
The clear white walls, a silver song
Which filled the house. He sang
The festive Chanuka songs:
"These Candles" and "Rock of Ages."
Later everyone sang the "Hymn of Dedication"
And then declared an intermission.
They immediately brought in a table
Laden with good things, enough to gladden the heart.
The women had baked for the holiday
Fragrant cakes,
And all kinds of sugar cookies.
They made chopped herring sprinkled
With the yolk and white of hard boiled eggs,
And fresh, fragrant chicken liver.
And in a happy holiday mood,
Flasks of brandy and fragile glasses sparkled.
When the women started serving,
The congregation made a hearty toast,
And everyone was delightfully cheerful.
The little ones unrestrained, played,
The women chattered loudly and
Dipped the brown honey-cake into brandy;
The Germans joined in the merriment,
Drank and ate and praised
The Lithuanian delicacies. Having eaten,
They all again became earnest,
But faces beamed with joy.
And eyes sparkled brightly.

When the cantor went up to the altar,
He started the singing for opening the Ark, and
It became like *Simkhas Torah* in the synagogue.
The men made *hakofes* with the Torah
And the cantor portioned out the honors.*
And every time the Torah scrolls
Passed the women, they bowed
And kissed the scrolls, holding children in their arms.

---

*Various tasks in connection with the handling and reading of the Torah scrolls.

The bells of the Torah crown tinkled,
And over the whole synagogue spread
Great happiness and peace and joy.
And after that the cantor began again:
"Guardian of Israel, oh, Guardian of Israel."
And the men, in one voice,
Joined with him,
And throughout the whole house spread
The happy sad defiant melody
Accompanied by humming and snapping of fingers:
"Let not Israel perish."
Suddenly, Max,
With great spirit and fire in his voice,
Jumped up to the new altar,
And started the familiar Yiddish song:
"Whatever we are, we are,
But Jews are we,"
And immediately the whole crowd joined in,
Old and young, women and children.
The stiff Germans also
Caught the ecstasy.
The song persisted,
Determined and strong, with faith and power.
The flames of the candles flickered,
Curling and stretching patterns
Overhead, like a deep fog,
Rising up to the high vaulted ceiling,
Which was no longer strange, but familiar and trustworthy.
High, fervent, and strong the words rang out:
"What we are, we are—
But Jews are we
What we do, we do—
But candles we bless!"

Six

A. Jacob

*C*lean-cut, firmly built, supple,
Tall, broad-shouldered, a strong chest,
His sturdy, muscular limbs
Clearly outlined beneath his immaculate clothing
Which fit as if poured.
Soft, black, shining hair
Falling in curls on his forehead,
The lips firm, resolute, and aggressive,
The eyes gray, sharp as his father's,
But young and laughing and free of sorrow,
Proud, full of self-assurance and self-worth.
These were the eyes
Of a strong, dominating character,
Which bends everything to its will
Without need of words.

He grew up in the new air
And was nurtured by another wind.
He did not know old complaints,
Ancient sorrows were not his.
He grew free, fresh, and handsome
With eyes open to a new life,
And ears avidly picking up
And absorbing the new sounds

Which were carried like a current,
Colorful, strong, gaudy, ringing,
Now tender, soothing, and caressing like silk,
Now sharp and raw, brutal and piercing.
The youth saw life face to face:
The red display of wild passion,
The atrocious, red fires,
The expression of man's hate,
Heard the hoof-beats of infuriated horses,
The frightening retort of distant guns,
And nightly drawn-out laments
Of women's voices, which pierce
The heart like sharp thin spears.
He saw the expression of the wild mob
On the accused black man:
The white rope around the black neck,
The black face gone gray, the mouth clenched,
The body convulsed in dread of death,
A small yellow fire smoldering at his feet,
The air filled with the smell and fumes of burnt flesh,
The yellowed white of the eyes rolling,
And blue lips pleading: "A bullet, a bullet,
Have pity. Shoot me!"
And he also saw the peace and tranquillity
Of the secure and strong young nation:
The great splendor of the summer market,
Which drowns in a sea of living flowers
And dots the face of field and garden with opulence.
The hot horses of the hot South,
And women's hot glances which, penetrating
The thin transparent veil
Of youthful modesty, say, "take me, take me."
As the seashell holds the sound of the sea,
His ears held the vibrations
Of sound and song and laughter,
Of friendly conversations and of angry words,
The cooing of doves overhead,
The strumming of big-bellied banjoes,
The trembling of soft mandolins,
The praise and glory to "Jesus-Lincoln"
Carried in ecstatic songs of old Negroes
Who still carried the marks
Of whips and chains, and gray brands

Burnt into the black skin as on horses.
The youth absorbed the sounds,
Color, and smell of the vast South
With its animals, people, fields, and woods:
The sweet juicy fragrant smell
Of the marvelous rich blue-grass,
The sweaty odor of lamb's wool
Packed in heavy bales after shearing,
The heat of summer days,
The coolness of dew drenched nights,
The mating calls of many birds,
And the pink tinged early morning stillness
On the distant furrowed tobacco fields,
The frosty winter mornings
With thick frozen chunks of ice,
When the whole city seems dipped
In the sharp, bittersweet smell
Of yellowed aging tobacco leaves
Loaded heavily on large flat wagons.

These, and thousands of other colors,
Sounds, and smells of the new fields
Filled the boy's heart and soul
With magical power,
Washed away the impressions of earliest childhood,
And suddenly, overnight, everything became new,
As if the old never existed.
The fresh impressions grew,
Rooted and strengthened in school,
And secured in the new ground.
The home soon lost its influence.
At first, his father still battled quietly,
Pitting himself against the new wind,
But later, gave up,
Becoming indifferent to everything except business.
Jake grew free and surrendered
To the instincts of a young heart.
He did very well in school,
Revealing a sharp clear mind,
He was part and parcel of his group,
Involved in physical play,
Taking pleasure in clever maneuvers.
But outside of school,

Books no longer interested him.
There was something too dead and frozen there.
Hot passion consumed him
And a burning desire for action and power.
When the young blood of friends
Heated by the Southern sun,
Began to surge,
With painful glowing desire,
They started secretly meeting
Blond, trembling, Gentile girls.
But something kept Jake back from this.
It was the ingrown feeling
Of a pure blood line, centuries old,
Which tamed the fire of his young blood
And guided him to expend himself
In other realms.
                    When he
Went right from school into his father's yard
It was with the full energy
Of a bubbling young body and soul.
He grew and matured in the yard.
He knew the value of every bit
Of raw leather and root and metal.
The pen served him; his head
Was quick, sharp, and receptive to business.
The respect which his father earned
After long, hard, strenuous years,
Came to him, the son, easily, effortlessly,
As naturally as if it belonged to him.
The neighbors held him in esteem,
Called him by his first name, attentively
Listened to young Jacob's word,
And secretly made a comparison
Between him and their own sons.
Something began to gnaw at them:
It was the dark feeling,
The heavy nebulous feeling, of one
Who had deluded himself,
But does not know how or where,
And can find no one to blame.
The Negroes, on the other hand, Sam, Tom, Humphrey,
And all the others who worked
In the yard, pulling, packing,

Sorting from early until late at night,
Accepted Jake's rule
Without questions and without misgivings.
They already recognized the master in him.
One look from Jacob was enough,
One word spoken, kindly but firmly,
Sent them scurrying into the corners
In the very middle of shrieking laughter.
Sam, who had a knack for breaking into a dance,
Remained standing, frozen in the middle
Of a lively number, smiling guiltily,
His eyes large, immobile, white,
Whenever Jake found him dancing
In the middle of work.
                              At home,
Jacob was looked up to as a leader.
Quiet, careful with words,
But with a friendly fatherly smile,
He seemed much older than the other children.
They deferred to him,
Felt in awe of him, listened
To his every word, and were elated
When they pleased their brother.
On Sunday evening, when
The young folk gathered in the house,
Jacob, friendly and gracious, entertained
His sister's friends and his own.
His tongue became free and sharp
And his tan face flamed
When, affectionately, he drew
His sister's blushing friend to him.
The father blew smelly clouds of smoke
From a black cigar,
And followed his son out of the corner of his eye
With pride and satisfaction.
Sometimes he would think: It's time
For him, the son, to build himself a home.
He would think of all the Germans
Who would be happy to have Jacob.
Recently, rich Hyman, winking, said
"He really gets things done, that Jake."
When the father, full of fatherly pride,
Kept quiet, the coarse Hyman

Gave Josh a nudge with his elbow,
And laughing, with devilish eyes,
Continued: "Okay, but what do you think
About my Flossie; she has a nice figure,
A good prudent housekeeper.
Ha-ha . . . What do you think?"

Thus

Jacob grew and matured,
But his heart was still free
And not touched by real passion for a woman
Until Vivian came into his life.

B. Vivian

*T*he first pioneers who
Cut their dreadful way through
The western side of Virginia and reached
The fertile region of the blue grass
Were truly heroes.
It was the striving of human nature,
The eagerness to discover new land,
Which drove the pioneers on
Cutting through the huge spiral mountains,
Stretching for hundreds of miles, covered
With dry, scrubby trees.
The pioneers did not know
About the wealth under their feet.
In the bowels of the yellow mountains
Were many rich treasures
Of hard, heavy, sparkling coal
And rich veins of black iron.
They looked for grass for their cattle,
And flat land to plow and sow.

The first to see the land of blue grass
For himself was Daniel Boone, the powerful, bold hunter.*
When Boone discovered
The rich soil of Kentucky,
He immediately sent a messenger to his brother

---

*Schwartz is taking poetic license. Boone was surely not the first to see Kentucky.

And all his relatives with the words:
"I discovered land, the grass is green and rich,
The plain is broad and wide, the water sweet,
Come. Let's settle this paradise."
And caravans started to move,
With oxen harnessed to covered wagons:
In the wagons
Children with thin pinched faces,
And open, eager eyes played.
With them were muscular, melancholy women,
Hardened in battle, like men.
They cut through mountains, and
After months of hardship, settled
Facing wind and cold, hunger and thirst,
And worst of all, the wild fury
Of battling tribes of Indians,
Who stalked them like wolves.
Sensing the beginning of the end,
The red man blocked their paths.
In his rage he spared no one,
Decorated himself with the scalps of the men,
Women, and children. The lucky ones who
Finally struggled through to the fertile land
Carried on their shoulders the burden
Of the needs and dangers of the new settlement:
Unsuccessful crops,
The frequent attacks of the enemy
With bows and arrows, tomahawks and fires.

The second generation was more relaxed.
The bloody wars stopped
And people worked in peace and freedom.
Flocks of sheep increased
And the plow glistened in the sun.
The women, still working like men
Among sheep and field,
Carried, nursed, buried,
And put the new generation on its feet.
They still looked like men,
With broad hands and feet and red faces,
But the stubborn gloom
Was gone and sometimes
Their mouths broke into a smile.
The women of the later generations

Were even softer and more feminine,
The fire of lust and desire in their blood
And in their clear worry-free eyes.
Careless laughter was on their lips.
The white males, masters
Of the fields, used whips
On the black man from hot Africa
Who poured his sweat into the rich earth.
A new nobility grew up
Of powerful, rich landowners
With tens and hundreds of servants.
A constant stream
Of luxuries from the whole world
Came into their fabulous castles and palaces:
Furs from Alaska and Siberia,
Wonderful, original satin and silk dresses
From Paris, the finest jewelry
Fashioned and engraved by goldsmiths,
Aged, bubbling champagnes,
The most expensive cigars from Havana,
White ostrich feathers from Africa.
Through time, the men
Became soft and effeminate like the women,
Their hands and faces white and languid,
Their lips made only for kissing.
They dressed in designer suits,
With fluttering ascots and wraps,
And like patricians from birth, devoted themselves
To art, to song, to Bacchus and Amor.

When the tough hewn plebian Lincoln arose,
Waving his sharp ax
With which, as a youth, he split wood
In the forests of his Kentucky home,
And when the ax undercut
The roots of their life,
The unruly, dispersed slaves
Guzzled the champagne
From their masters' cool cellars
And paraded on naked black feet
In their mistresses sable furs,
White ostrich feathers on black heads.
The younger, stronger ones awakened
And faced a new life

Under new circumstances. The weaker,
Under stress, lost their heads,
Gave up rich, fertile plantations,
Sold out their castles and estates,
For whatever they could get, headed
Towards wherever their eyes led them.
Still others went to their rest
In poor squalid quarters
Of London and Paris, died beggars,
Drunk on cheap absinthe.
Years later, many dragged themselves
Back home, so that their spent bodies
Could be laid in their native, faithful earth.

From one of these very families,
Vivian was conceived.
She just barely remembered her parents
As if in a distant faded dream.
Yet some memory remained
In her mind, like a pale golden beam.
The child was raised by her uncle,
An aristocratic, small landowner.
She grew, a young seedling,
Eyes bright like cornflowers,
Golden-red curls of soft hair,
Slender, shapely, supple limbs.
And this girl was
A mixture and synthesis of all the generations:
The strength and determination of the pioneers,
The sunniness, tenderness, and exuberance
Of generations raised in serenity.
When the girl started coming
To the Jew's house, a friend
Of his daughters, the whole house
Came alive, and alive with Vivian.
The girls seemed as if under a spell,
The elder Josh delighted in the fresh
Silvery, sparkling laughter.
It made him younger.
Even the old woman smiled,
The creases on her face happily
Dissolving. And Jacob couldn't
Take his eyes off the girl.

At first, he didn't dare
Get close to Vivian, but later
He felt more comfortable with her.
He invited her to the Sunday evening dances,
And his heart beat with a painful sweetness, beat
When he nervously drew her to him.
Under the tan skin of his face
His blood throbbed hot with desire.

With time the friendship grew,
The differences between them an attraction,
Something new, fresh, and exciting.
As the fresh spring earth absorbs
The first fragrant spring rain,
Their young desirous hearts
Absorbed the fresh stream
Of bubbling, rushing feelings.
Before their hearts
Understood where they were drifting,
The two were already dreaming,
Carried on a stream of pink waves,
Charmed, lulled, by the tender feelings
Which occupied and spun their lives.

Thus some time passed,
Until, one fine day, the pair
Went to the old, good-natured pastor
And married.

C. In-Laws

*O*ld Josh, with a cigar in his mouth,
Sat quietly and controlled,
His eyes smarting from the smoke,
His gray head sunk into his shoulders.
He heard and didn't hear the old neighbor
With the pointed tremulous beard
And the small beady blue eyes.
The neighbor spoke sedately, quietly,
Let the smoke from the black pipe curl,
Tried to look into the Jew's eyes.
But the Jew squinted because of the smoke,

119

And it was impossible for the neighbor
To see and to understand the Jew's mind,
Which worried the neighbor greatly.
The "Uncle Sam" beard nervously trembled,
And the sparse gray hairs
Of the old head fluttered.
The old woman in the black silk dress
Sat stiff and straight in her chair,
In one and the same pose, as if frozen,
Her eyes veiled, lifeless, heavy.
The lamp over the table burned brightly,
Reflecting thin clear flames
In the glasses of strong tea which no one
Even touched to his lips.
Ashamed, the tea, cooled,
Raising thin wreaths of steam.
And the wall clock ticked, ticked,
And spread gloom within the house.

The neighbor finally ran out of patience
And from a thinly disguised tone
Came bitterness and gall.
Hostility blazed in his eyes,
His thin blood in
The old skull with the sparse hair
Spread a dismal redness
Under the wrinkled parchment skin.
He banged the table with all his strength
So that the old woman jumped, startled.
His voice became sharp and cutting,
And looking hard into the Jew's face
He spoke grimly: "Josh," he said,
"When the girl came and said
That she married your son,
I couldn't believe my ears.
My brother's daughter, and the Jew? A fine pair.
If my brother Howard were alive
It probably wouldn't have come to this.
I've been going around the last few months confused.
I am ashamed to raise my eyes.
So what do I find out? You are angry.
You drove your son out of the business.
And who can we complain to. To live to see this!"

Quietly and coolly the Jew responded
"And I? I was certainly not looking for such lineage."
"Is that so!" The neighbor became more incensed.
"I didn't even want to come here.
I can't expect any respect from you.
But I like the way you, Josh, are so arrogant.
I'd only like, Josh, to know the secret
Of your great and noble lineage.
Is it in the fact that your forefathers
Nineteen hundred years ago
Crucified Jesus?"
    The Jew didn't answer:
The cigar in his hand went dead.
With his other hand, he covered
His weary eyes, as if he were asleep.
Each angry, harsh word
Hit him like a sharp stone
And his skin smarted with pain.
Lost in thought and suffering intensely
In the large, deep chair, he kept silent.

The neighbor waited for an answer,
Struck matches to light his pipe,
But the matches broke
And he angrily put the pipe away.
When he could wait no longer
He began to talk again,
"Well, Josh,
Do you, at least, remember how you came here?
A beggar, a gypsy, tattered,
Who wandered down all the roads,
Thin, emaciated, with a load on your back.
And now you are fat, Josh, and smooth,
With houses and warehouses and money."
(Regards the house with pointed looks,
Spreads his hands, and storms anew:)
"Established yourself a bit, with silk and satin,
Silver and gold, with all good things.
Half of the city belongs to you already.
I would say that you, at least, should be appreciative.
Should be thankful for your good fortune.
But no. You're ungrateful and withdrawn.
My brother's daughter is not good enough for you.

What does it say in your Old Testament?
When Jeshurun waxed fat, he kicked."
The old woman sat the whole time,
Sat stiff and quiet and as if frozen,
But silent tears welled up
In her red eyes.
They ran down her pale face,
Coursing past her nose and lifeless lips,
And from the lips they fell onto her heart.
Throughout this time, she didn't move,
Didn't wipe her running eyes.
Didn't speak, didn't sob, didn't stir.
She just drenched herself with silent tears.
When the neighbor finally finished
Josh took his hand away from his face.
(His face was distorted with sorrow
And his eyes blazed angrily.)
He straightened himself in his chair, and said:
"Did you say everything that's on your chest, neighbor?
If you were not my daughter-in-law's uncle
I would not put up with your crudeness.
Out of respect for her I spared you.
You throw up to me my plight of long ago,
And to this day you don't approve of me.
No doubt, this is green-eyed jealousy.
Poverty, people say, is no shame.
And if now half the city belongs to me,
As you wish to have it, I struggled and worked
Long years for all of it.
But this isn't what I want to tell you:
You mentioned in passing before
The old sin of my ancient forefathers,
That they crucified your God. That
Was perhaps the first reason
Why I did not want your brother's daughter.
It's possible, years from now, that when
The heat of young passion will cool,
That he, my son, will hear the same
From the mouth of his own wife, his flesh and blood,
And that would be too horrible. But, furthermore,
You needn't worry about Jacob.
Jake will take care of himself.
Good night, neighbor."

Seven

A. Children

*T*hese are the names of the children
   Of old Josh and Sarah, his wife:
Jacob, Lionel, Edwin and Willard—the sons,
Dorothy, Diana, and Ethel—the daughters.
Except for Jacob, the foreign born,
None of them needed
To be Americanized. They were born
Into the new world as citizens, proud, free,
And conducted themselves as such.
       Lionel:
Lionel grew up a law abiding man,
Fat, sedate, peaceful.
He pushed through school with difficulty;
And his father put him to work
In the big red warehouse next to the old scale:
He stood there and supervised the weighing,
Making sure the balance did not tip
This way or that; he weighed rags,
Bales of wool, feathers, horsebones,
Rusty old gray iron,
And fresh hot bloody skins.
Lionel had a right to brag
Because he never made a mistake.
He stood by the scale

Until he grew into a young man
Slightly round shouldered
From so much bending and bowing towards the scale.
When Jacob, consulting no one,
Married Vivian,
Josh brought together
Lionel and Flossie, Hyman's girl.
The pair "courted" a little while.
And then had a large wedding
With much fanfare: the rich, stingy Hyman
Grunted, groaned, bargained,
But his devices didn't work.
He lavishly supplied a house
With furniture, carpets, and a piano.
At dawn, the day after the wedding,
Lionel came into the yard
And took up his usual place near the scale.
        Edwin:
After Lionel, came the brother Edwin.
This Edwin was a youth in perpetual motion:
Handsome, bright, nervous and quick.
But there was something in his nature
Which prevented him from adapting himself
To anything useful. He was a devil,
He managed ball games spiritedly
And high-handedly; still a boy,
He carried on with lively Gentile girls
For nights on end. His father punished him,
His mother begged and cried,
But none of the arguments helped:
That mischief-maker was on fire, and that was that.
He became a compulsive gambler:
Gambled on cards, gambled on dice,
Gambled on horses in hot races.
When the horses left the city,
Edwin was not too lazy to follow
This splendid amusement wherever it occurred:
Louisville, Atlanta, New Orleans.
His mother called him "quicksilver,"
And his father called him worse.
Once, when Josh was not cautious enough,
Edwin took advantage of the opportunity
To lay his hands on a large sum of money.

124

No one saw him again.
Occasionally regards came
From green gambling tables
Or sunny, blossoming Florida, or
From distant San Francisco.
The last word they had of him
Was from white, snow-covered Alaska,
Where Edwin went, joining the stream of prospectors
To look for gold among the ice and snow.
         Willard:
This brother, Willard, did not like
The scrap business. Willard was
Withdrawn, quiet by nature.
He diligently went through school and high school,
And then his old father, Josh,
Allowed him to study in the large city.
Willard studied medicine
And came back home a doctor.
He was held in high esteem by the neighbors,
And they greeted him from a distance
With "Good morning, Doc!" Willingly
The sick came to him to be cured.
The neighbors had an expression:
"Just as the father is lucky,
So is the son."
Later, he brought home a wife from the distant city.
She lived apart from everyone,
Did not become too friendly with anyone,
As is fitting for a young doctor's wife.
Once she came into the junkyard.
The old man showed her around,
Trying to point out and explain things to her.
But she was squeamish, held a perfumed
Handkerchief tightly to her nose. They could
Never again entice her to set foot there.
         Dorothy:
The oldest of the daughters: tall and slender,
A good student, like all daughters,
Read much and played the piano,
Possessed spirit and a quick mind,
Was the life of her circle.
When the incident with Jacob occurred,
The elder Josh sent her away

To a relative in Chicago:
Let the girl mingle with Jews there.
She married a man in Chicago,
And, according to the gossip in town,
Lived like a princess.
Several years later, Dorothy
Came back to her father's house
In black, in mourning, tall and slim,
Her face pale and transparent, like a Madonna's,
With blue rings around her deep eyes.
She brought with her little David,
With thin hands and feet
And a radiant expression in his large eyes.
The town talked, told stories
Of big speculations in the city,
And of a final bullet in the head.
But they were never able to verify it.
Dorothy loyally observed widowhood.
For years she did not touch the piano,
Became religious, and Friday nights
Her pair of candles burned opposite her mother's.
Into the house of old Josh
Came new books
Of Jewish history, and religion,
The poems of the gentle Emma Lazarus
And others. In the town, the talk was
That Dorothy wanted to be a rabbi:
She studied the holy language from the *Khumesh*.
    Diana:
When Dorothy came back home,
Diana left:
She married a rich merchant
From a new, nearby community.
Her life was full, quiet, and peaceful
And each time that she came home
She had something new to show:
A diamond ring, a locket, or earrings.
Her fat face shone with well-being.
And she never tired of telling
About Herman's generosity and courtesy,
And how her Herman would
Risk his life for her.

Ethel:
Capricious like a small spoiled child,
With long, thin and nervous fingers,
She would dream her days away at the piano.
Once, when raw life touched her,
Her young being shut, closed
Like a sleeping flower closes
When oncoming night starts to fall.
In town there was talk of tragic love.
The household attended her
As one attends a delicate, sickly child,
Fulfilling her smallest wish, her least desire.
In the pink evening, she went for a drive
Outside of town, in a small carriage
Harnessed to a frisky pony.
When she came back home
Her whole young being was fragrant
With wild field flowers, dew, and summernight.
In her soft wandering glance
Flickered something strange and distant,
Incomprehensible and other worldly.
When Dorothy came home
Bringing her son, the little David,
Ethel awoke, as from a sleep.
The house rang with the sound
Of her melodious, lovely, strong young voice.
She never left the side of the child
And was like a mother to him.
Both sisters, tall and thin and shapely,
One in black, the other in white,
Attended the child like two mothers.

B. Death

*M*eanwhile life continued
Like the old clock on the wall.
And everyone was occupied
With his own worries, experiences, dreams.
Young grandchildren were born,
And on a holiday
The house was full of sons and daughters,

Dressed up little boys and girls
With brown, blond, and black heads,
Sleepy heavy faces,
And happy impish faces.
Now, the old woman often did not know
Whose child was around her legs,
Or what his name was.
Old age weighed her down.
She distributed candy and cookies among them,
But seldom ran her hand
Over the soft hair of young heads.

She died as she lived:
Quiet, becalmed, without complaints.
Sons and daughters encircled her,
But in the last quiver of agony
She fixed her dismal look
On her husband, and turned away no more.
Long after she expired,
He was still under the burden
Of her heavy, dismal glassy look.

Later, the house filled with quiet,
Smells of death, yellow candles,
And heavy, overwhelming bouquets of flowers.
The old woman lay in the coffin
Dressed up in a full, black silk dress.
Under the thick black veil
Her gray hair looked like silver.
The yellow death candle was reflected
In the old, golden wedding ring
On her thin dead hand.
The whole city milled around the house:
The old gray neighbors who still
Remembered this Josh from other times,
The younger who traded with him
In the businesses and banks,
The sisters' friends and acquaintances,
The same old pastor with the mild face,
The busy harried Litvaks
With wives and children, who didn't know
What to do with their hats—
Whether or not to take them off.

To Litvaks the whole ceremony
Of the prayer seemed peculiarly foreign.
The young, thin rabbi, dressed in black,
Stiffly buttoned up to the neck,
His face smooth shaven, his head bare,
Glistening glasses on his eyes,
Read in an appropriate tone.
Smooth polished words
From a thin, black-bound Book of Psalms
Fell like jewels:
Familiar words, but in a new tongue,
Which disturbed all hearts.
"God, our Master, how great is Thy name
Over the world:
Who hast shown Thy splendor
In the heavens.
When I see Thy heavens,
The work of Thy fingers,
Moon and stars which Thou hadst secured,
What is man that Thou art mindful of him,
And the son of man, that Thou shoulds't remember him?"
He paused, quiet for a few moments.
In the quiet strained house
The leafing of thin pages was heard.
He began reciting anew
The prayer of Moses, the Godly man:
" . . . Even before the hills were born,
And before Thou hadst created earth and world,
Thou wast already God, forever and forever."
And further:
"Like withered grass . . . which sprouts in the dawn
And dries and withers in the evening.
All our days disappear in Thy wrath . . . "

The old man heard and didn't hear:
Time and motion stopped
As in a hazy, convoluted dream,
And everything was mixed with that dismal look:
The sons and daughters and the dead face,
The unreal light of the yellow candles,
The heavy odor of the flower wreaths,
The face of the young, unfamiliar rabbi,
Who sadly drew out monotones.

Minutes stretched to eternity,
And the whole of life lasted a moment.
In another moment, the past
Disappeared and dissolved like smoke.
So he tried to listen to the voice.
He was able to recognize familiar words.
Familiar, but yet estranged.
He went back to the past,
To the thought which did not let go,
The ancient thought, from the beginning of time,
Since the first man started to think:
What is the purpose and the sense of it all?
Then the nightmare began again:
The familiar streets of the city
Were now unfamiliar and strange,
The fields, the grass, and then the tombstones,
And fresh graves covered with flowers.
So many white marble figures—
And crosses, crosses, crosses everywhere.
A large, red, fiery sun was
Motionless in the sky.
He woke at the edge of the grave
Which smelled of fresh, cool earth,
And he came to himself, as from a dream:
The coffin had been lowered into the grave
And the rabbi bowed over it
Reading again from the little black book.
But here, in the open field,
In the presence of quiet eternal life,
The voice sounded sorrowful, lost.
The rabbi threw white flowers in the grave,
Bending over it, saying:
"Dust thou art, to dust returnest."
And when the earth started to fall
With heavy thumping sounds on the cover of the coffin,
Josh remembered another winter day,
When he and she, now in her grave,
Had chopped open a grave
For their young dead child.
Falling on top of the little mound
Which was now green and peaceful,
Covered with grass and wild field flowers,
He wanted to cry to their child
That she, the mother, had joined her.

But he could not speak.
As he lay upon the grave, his well
Of hot tears opened.
And he sobbed out loud
Like a small and helpless child.

C. Evening Shadows

*O*ver the mother's sick bed,
Father and son had made their peace.
From the first day, Josh had missed his son.
Yet, too proud to show his feelings,
He had remained silent. And so had his son.
But by the mother's bed, and later on at the funeral,
It was easy to say friendly words
Which came honestly from the heart:
The business needed young blood;
Strong competitors had sprung up;
And old Josh felt that it was
Too hard for him, that his strength was
Not up to carrying the heavy burden alone.
He knew very well that Lionel
Would not go far: although good at the scale,
He could not be depended upon for more.
One day, without mincing words,
He asked Jacob to come back to the place,
And Jacob didn't take long to decide.
He immediately accepted his father's proposition.
And on the sign near the large old house
"And Son" was added.

Life continued
On its daily, prescribed route.
Busy from early morning till late at night
With trade and merchandise and litigations,
Profits and losses, the old man
Now often found business hard
And tedious. He yearned
To withdraw from the whole thing
And to dream somewhere quietly.
He tried to remain in the house,
But the quiet of the house did not agree with him.
He once even searched out

Old *Reb Bakhye* from the dust,
But *Reb Bakhye* now left him cold:
It was not what he wanted. He returned to the place
And harnessed himself again to the yoke,
Even though he knew that it was unnecessary,
That Jacob could manage very well without him.
But to be superfluous in God's world
Was not his nature. So, again,
With heart and soul, he threw himself
Into his business and remained thus
Occupied, concerned. The only ones who
Now lightened his heavy gloom were
Vivian, his daughter-in-law,
His melancholy daughters at home,
And the fragile child David.

Vivian often came into the place
Bringing her little girl:
Slight, gentle, laughing,
Charming dimples in her face.
She carried a new fragrance into the place
Entrancing him with her fresh youth.
She kissed the old man on the forehead,
And childishly carefree, snuggled close to him.
He loved taking her around,
Showing her the place, and explaining things to her.
She listened earnestly to him,
Chattering childishly,
Something of her freshness remained
Long after she had left the place,
A bunch of fresh, blue-violet lilacs,
Or crisp wild roses at summer's end.

Although Josh's day was then drawing towards a close,
There was still strength in his loins,
His eye was still sharp, flashing,
And sometimes a cheerful little flame
Would glow in them. But evening shadows
Engulfed his heart.
Later, when the old woman's grave was
Overgrown with tall grass,
He would, on sunny free days,
Come to visit her. The field was

Bright and inviting;
Crosses and tombstones sparkled,
Shimmering peacefully in the hot sun.
The stillness was so large and deep,
That the very silence spoke,
With quiet joy it seeped into the weary heart.
One half of the old woman's headstone
Was already written upon, engraved
With golden letters; the other half,
Smooth, shining, and polished,
Reflecting the mixed colors
Of grass and trees, sunlight and shadows,
Waited for that unknown day
When the gravestone scribe would come
To engrave a new name into the stone.
It was peculiarly endearing and sad
At the same time: to know certainly and surely
That further than here one cannot go,
That here, just here, under this mound, is
The end of every beginning, the end of all ends.

D. Life

*Y*outh lived its full life:
    Days became weeks,
Months were linked into years;
And day, and week, and month were full
Of secret promises for the future.
Each year brought something new,
A new expectation, a new joy,
In the first flutter within a mother's body,
In the first helpless cry of the child,
In the first sweet, innocent smile,
And in the first steps
Of little babies.

       At first the years
Were hard and lean. There was need in the house
And Jake could not adapt himself to anything.
It was hard for him, with his nature,
To work for someone else.
But need breaks iron. Later, with time,

133

He somehow became reconciled
And made peace with his lot.
Vivian intuitively understood
How to make the poverty pleasant,
How to light up every corner.
The small house was full
Of the warmth of young love.
Sometimes the girls, Jacob's sisters,
Came to visit and the house
Echoed fresh joyfulness
And young hearty laughter.
When the first child arrived
The house filled with new happiness,
Childish cries, satisfied noises,
And the young mother's voice
That lulled the baby to sleep.
In the summer the small house greened
Among trees one hundred years old,
Smelled of wild field flowers and lilacs
In early spring. Later, wild fragrant
June roses blossomed,
Climbed up the walls over the veranda
And onto the old roof. Sunflowers
On thick green stalks bloomed brightly,
Shaking heads of yellow flowers,
And revealing thick black rows
Of ripening seeds. In winter
Every fireplace in the house burned.
The large, broad field covered with snow
And trees covered with dull silver
Could be seen from the small window.
At night, it was lovely to hear
The sad sound of the branches,
And the night howl of the wind.
Inside, the house was warm and cozy.
The infant gurgled and bubbled
Happily, in warmth and plenty,
In its crib in the corner.

Vivian who was religiously inclined
Went to church
Every Sunday and returned inspired.
With large, moist, gleaming eyes

She would quickly repeat to Jake
The pastor's new sermon,
And some sentiment which moved her.
She often reproached him: Why
Was he so indifferent to faith?
How can one live without God?
Later on, she somehow obtained
Two old brass candlesticks, and on Fridays
When Jacob came back home,
He would find two candles burning,
Fresh *hallahs* and red wine.
She would dress herself in white
And the feeling of Sabbath was in the house.
She implored him to teach her
The blessing for the lighting of the candles,
But Jacob had to confess
That he had never known it.
She became more endearing than ever to him.

Afterwards, when Jacob returned
To his old father, prosperous
Years came, not extravagant,
Modest, but there was plenty in the house,
And his head was free from worry.
Vivian, drawing closer to the old man,
Became like a daughter to him.
Often the father joked
That she, Vivian, was more Jewish
Than his daughters, that Jewishness attracted her.
True, she never missed a Sunday
At church, and made sure that the child
Went to the old pastor for Sunday school,
But Friday night she lit candles.
And on *Rosh Hashana* and *Yom Kippur* she came
To the synagogue together with old Josh,
Her husband, and her young child.
The Litvaks were astonished,
And quietly whispered to each other.
It was hard to understand such a thing.
Finally Jacob got sick of it
And started to plan a temple,
A temple with an organ and a rabbi.
The Germans immediately joined in,

And old Josh was caught up in it.
The congregation split;
The temple was built.
Every Friday, at sundown,
The organ pealed its zealous celebration,
And the choir of young girlish voices
Rang out from the high, lighted niche,
And out on the distant street
Came the incantation: *Shma-Yisroel*!

Eight

A. Years Later

*W*hen David grew up and became a man
His grandfather Josh, already old,
Was growing in the other direction,
Small, quiet, shrunken,
His face wrinkled and yellow,
His eyes cloudy, lifeless and cold,
The hair on his head and beard yellowed from age.
The Negro in a limousine
Drove him daily, morning and evening,
To and from the place.
It was sad, pitiful,
To see the shriveled old man
Nestling quietly, lost
In the deep seat of the large limousine.

Half in earnest, half in jest, the old man
Would say: The day on which I don't appear
At this place will be my last.
He even came on the stormy days
Of cold winter, when earth and sky
Twisted and merged,
And in the heat of summer,
When a fiery sun baked the earth
From a burning, glowing sky,

In the bright clear days of spring,
And in the darkened, weeping autumn days.
For all appearances, he still came to work,
But in winter he slept away the day
By the warmth of the glowing coal stove,
And in summer, when the Southern sun burned,
He baked at the south wall
Of the large red building, sighing out loud,
And puffing on an old black pipe.
In his heart, the old man knew
That he really needn't come,
Anymore. He was in the way.
And it would have been more sensible to go home,
To sleep, to rest, and maybe
Even to look, sometimes, into a holy book.
But the red building lured him,
Had complete power over him.
As an old, retired dog
Comes home to lie on his master's threshold
So did Josh, in his second childhood,
Return to the security of his building.

Time passed, monotonously and quietly.
It really made no difference
How one killed it.
He was warmed by the sun in summer,
And in winter, the burning stove warmed him.
But what then? In summer one was freer.
A man can hide outdoors
And smoke his pipe in private.
Indoors, in the big red house,
He no longer felt free.
He was somehow superfluous. Outdoors, occasionally,
An old, retired neighbor came along.
And they would sit, comfortable in the hot sun,
Talking over the good old times
When the world was better,
The sun shone more brightly,
And life had a different flavor.
And if no neighbor came, it didn't matter.
There was always old Sam,
The first Negro
To work for him in the old days.

Sam was also retired, but for appearances' sake,
Still earned his bread.
Sam was all bones, never still,
His shining lively face
Fitted into a white frame,
A thick, grizzly white beard which
Made the black face look younger.
It was as if Sam, performing a childish trick,
Had whitewashed his beard,
Or had crept out of a sack
Of fresh white flour. They sat for days
And told each other all kinds of stories.
When Sam was in high spirits, he sang
Church spirituals,
Told Josh stories of slavery,
Fairy tales, a whole "Thousand and One Nights."
The old man shook his head in disbelief,
He sensed that not everything Sam told
Had to be accepted as the pure truth;
He intuitively felt that now and then Sam
Peppered and salted with a liberal hand.
Yet he fell under Sam's spell:
Winked slyly with one eye while the other sparkled
With the wisdom of age.
He stroked his old yellowed white beard,
And with relish began to tell a story himself.
But Sam could not be fooled either.
Sam understands that old Josh tells
Him stories that are entirely untrue:
The ghosts are no ghosts,
The devils are no devils.
For some reason the old boss
Wants to enjoy a good story.
So let him. Whom does it bother? Sam pretends
That the story frightens him to death,
Rolls his large, young looking eyes,
And crosses himself in feigned fear
Until, at last, old Josh breaks out
In a satisfied cackle,
And Sam pretends that he is insulted.

Sometimes, the old boss awakens in him:
Suddenly he gets angry at the Negro,

And drives old Sam to work.
From out of thin air he learns that the business
Is going downhill without supervision.
And God only knows where
That dried-up, little, skinny ancient
Gets so much energy. Josh runs with quick small steps
From one end of the large building to the other.
He is in every corner, poking in the wool,
Rooting among the yellow bones and iron,
Chewing on a piece of ginseng.
He sees feathers spilled from a sack
Flying in the street,
He flies after them like a hen,
Calling out in a thin, squeaky voice,
And collects the feathers one by one.
The Negroes come out to help him.
They go hunting, leaving their work,
And are afraid to laugh out loud.
And Lionel, who is now fat and gray,
Runs to the office to tell Jacob
About what is going on. When Jacob arrives
He finds things topsy-turvy on the yard.
The Negroes move in circles as in a dance,
The father's anger comes out in shrieks.
Jacob smiles, talks quietly to his father,
Calms him and leads him to the office.
The old man, however, is not quieted for long;
He pitches and thrashes like a stubborn child
Until Jacob can't stand it and leaves.
Then Josh sits down to dictate letters to customers;
The girl takes her notebook and pencil
And smiling, looks at him with surprise.
The old man looks at her with angry eyes
And indulges himself in a little dig:
Flour, that is, her powder, must have
Fallen in price in the country. The girl
Bites her red, painted lips.
The old man starts to dictate, beginning quietly,
But the old boss within him starts talking louder,
Becoming eager, and banging his fist on the table.
A moment later, the fire is gone,
He forgets where he is, his look becomes blank.
The girl yawns, waits patiently,

140

And winks slyly to a friend.
The old man wakes from the empty dream,
And hardly has the patience to finish.
Later, when the girl brings him
The letter, typed on the office machine,
He puts his glasses on
And signs his name with a feeble hand.
Still later, when the letter is brought
To Jacob, he throws it
Into the basket under the desk. Old Sam,
Who sees everything from beginning to end,
Is aggravated
And shakes his white head,
His faithful eyes blinking.
It is not nice to do this to an old boss.

Josh's life really consisted
Of one long chain of habits
And little nothings. There was nothing
In the future which might attract him,
No bright mirage to delude
And enchant his lifeless eyes.
He lived for the moment, came
Into the old place daily, pushed through the day,
Went back to his quiet corner,
Where he felt himself to be important.
Indifferently, passively, he accepted
The care and small tendernesses
Of his two, now faded, daughters.
And it was sad, how his soul
Dried up with his body:
From the former merchant with the clear look
And a concern for many things and subjects,
He now became a very stingy old man
Who shook over every penny.
God knows where he had found
The faded, mouldy pouch
Which hung around his neck on a string.
On market-day he went out
To buy provisions for the house.
The market knew him: a bad penny.
He wandered among the wagons,
Bargained desperately with the farmers,

And, with shaking hands,
He counted the slippery coins
For the first, the second, and the third time,
Avarice and distrust flashing
In his small, sharp eyes.

Thus appeared old Josh
When he already had one foot
In that grave waiting beside his wife's.

B. Children's Children

A tree," philosophizes Sam,
    Has millions of leaves; each leaf
Is different from another and unique.
And if anyone can prove the reverse,
Sam is ready to eat the leaves."
So says Sam. And he says this
Apropos of children. In addition, Sam brings
Evidence from a verse in the Bible:
"A person is like a tree in the field."
Old Josh thinks differently, however.
He thinks that all have one face,
And all are out for his "mazuma."
In fact, he has now forgotten the number
Of his grandchildren. Jacob
Has so many and so many, Lionel so many,
The doctor and the smooth, fat daughter
Are not far behind either. He starts to count,
But he doesn't have enough fingers on his hands,
And he stops in the middle. In addition, it seems to him
That all these "rabbit eaters" have only
One thing in mind, sports and automobiles.
Somehow they grow as if on yeast
And every moment there is another celebration.
A grandchild becomes engaged and is married,
And immediately another one copies him.
Indeed, it appears to him that the whole purpose
Of these frequent celebrations is in order
To milk him, the allegedly rich grandfather.
They do it on purpose. Let the grandfather
Show up with the expensive presents.

Presents, contends old Josh,
Are indeed superfluous. In his time
Who paid attention to gold and silver?
Who cared about pianos? You want to marry?
Go buy a simple wooden bed,
Two or three chairs, a table, and a pot,
And be finished with this business. But in the end
His contentions and his arguments are of no help.
Groaning sadly, he gives, of course. What can he do?

And yet, he gets pleasure from a celebration:
A world, a world, a dressed-up world
Of sons and daughters, daughters-in-law and sons-in-law.
And grandchildren of all ages,
With new, growing, busy little ones.
It shimmers and whispers with satin and silk,
Earrings and pearls on necks glitter,
Diamonds sparkle on fingers and in hair.
A jubilant world! Josh forgets himself,
He is seated at the head table
And all woo him and are proud of him.
The best portion is brought to him,
And when the rabbi rises to say a word,
He invariably praises old Josh,
The wise and clever patriarch.
The old man is moved to tears,
Overwhelmed by the wine and praise.
But on the morrow the wine and praise wear off
And the distrust returns.
With a shaking hand, he writes
In a certain book especially for that purpose
How much the new celebration cost him.

The Negro sticks to his own opinion:
He says that as certain as it is that God made
Small green apples—so is it certain
That each one is a world unto himself,
With his good and bad points and inclinations.
And if the fable about the tree is not enough,
He also brings in more evidence: dogs.
(Old Sam, like his whole race,
Is a connoisseur and lover of dogs.)
He argues: If a dog is different

And by nature, distinct from another,
Then even more so a human, who walks on two legs.
And when old Josh thinks more deeply,
He admits that the Negro is right.
(Obviously, he doesn't tell him that.)
He accepts this opposite view
When he thinks with a clear head
About his two dear grandchildren.

The first is his Jacob's daughter Flora.
The best proof is that when the old man
Was in a sad mood
He needed only to see her, and immediately his face
Acquired an entirely different expression.
His eyes lit up.
She had a lot of her father's strength,
And yet much of her mother's womanliness and charm.
She was religious and quiet,
As is usual for sensitive children
Of Jewish-Christian marriages.
She went regularly to church,
But would also visit the synagogue
On Fridays and on Jewish holidays.
And both religions were good.
Nor did one interfere with the other.
Of course, the Christian legends
Had a greater influence on the girl at first,
But later the old God Jehovah
Was helped along by the young rabbi.
The young rabbi with the ascetic face
Honestly, enthusiastically, believed in
Israel's mission among the nations.
He taught Flora Jewish history
And the basic tenets of the old faith.
He put his soul into his faith,
Read her mystical-religious poems
From the passionate, yearning *Ben Gavirol,**
And his fiery words
Made her young heart tremble.
Jehovah won, together with the rabbi:

---

*Leading Hebrew poet and philosopher of the Spanish period.

The friendship blossomed into a love,
Which led them to marriage.
As indifferent as the old man had been,
He now was joyful and eager as a child.
At the wedding, Josh was
The happiest of all the in-laws.
His old eyes shone
With a true, youthful, clear light,
His tongue moved with sharp wit.
He talked about the great good fortune when blood
Is not estranged from its own source.
He tried to bring in evidence from Scripture,
Caressed Vivian and Jacob, his son,
And warm, quiet tears
Fell from his old eyes.
She, Flora May, was one
Of his two beloved grandchildren.
The other was the young David,
Dorothy's son.

C. David

*T*he gentle little boy with the brown eyes
    And fine head of curly chestnut hair
Did not grow up effeminate
Despite the soft, warm wings
Of two mothers who loved him.
They worried about him,
Demanded complete obedience from him,
Did not allow him to take a step without their knowledge.
Yet, in spite of that, the young boy
Slipped out from under their hands,
Getting lost for a day, coming
Home late. When the mothers,
Frightened and weeping,
Fell upon the child with punishment and tenderness,
He put them off with laughter.
Proud and free, with a sense of independence,
He told them where he was,
What he saw, and what he thought.
Sometimes, he would disappear beyond the city
In the open fields and woods, and come back

Dirty, scratched, torn
By brambles, white cobwebs
Twisted in his brown curls.
For the most part he was attracted to people
In the city's crowded streets.
He was an unusual being
Who, with all his fine senses,
Smelled the air, and felt as if intoxicated
By even the gentlest breeze. Instinctively
He felt the pain and suffering of the weak,
And the helplessness of the injured.
One day he returned from the street,
His face convulsed with pain.
His brown eyes were large,
And burning feverishly with anger.
It was hard at first to find out
What had happened to him. But later,
When he somehow regained his composure,
The whole household was able to picture the market,
The tavern at the corner, the drunken Negro
Who accidentally brushed against a white man,
The murderous face of the white man,
With his raised bottle of whiskey in the air.
The sound of glass rang in their ears,
And before their eyes stood the Negro
Propping himself up against a wall, then slowly
Collapsing onto the sidewalk. They saw
The black face blue with suffering and pain,
Rivulets of blood mixing with
Rivulets of whiskey, nearby
His old hat, broken,
Stepped on and spat upon by the white.
His large eyes suddenly sobered
With the agony of a persecuted dog.
Everyone clearly heard the painful cry
From the Negro's blue lips: "Jesus, Jesus."
David's mother shook as if in fever,
His aunt Ethel put her hands to her heart,
And both, with one voice, cried out
That it was dangerous for the young boy
To be exposed to
The harmful, poisonous street.
Old Josh, however, who was younger

Then, and understood things,
Interceded for the youth,
Arguing that the evil of the street
Would not stick to the boy.
On the contrary, he thought that raw life
Would have a strengthening influence
On the delicate nature of the boy.
Knowing the difference between good and evil,
He would be able to look at life
With thoughtful independent eyes.
And the old man was right.
The youth grew up free and brave,
Knew intuitively how to separate
The wheat from the chaff. His self-respect
Did not permit him to be mean
Or petty. The affluence of the house
Made him independent, not avaricious.
His understanding of things and events
Was clear and sharp beyond his years.
All his actions and feelings
Were dictated by one concept: justice.
Later, when the youth was grown,
The teachings and ideas of thinkers
Were no revelation to him.
With their words, they merely confirmed
The inner voice of his young heart
Which yearned for the good. The books
Helped bring out the best
And the brightest in his young being.
Since his heart was open
And his ideas ingenuous,
Learning was easy and effortless.
He often surprised the teacher
With his simple, but profound, words.
It was as if the spring of Torah
Which was dammed up by his grandfather
Was opened again by the young sapling
And began flowing freely, clearly,
With the ancient wisdom
Of generations of elders whose life was steeped
In the house of Torah.
                          The mother wanted
The son to be a rabbi. But the son

Was not thinking about practical things.
He studied in the large distant city,
Loved by the rabbi, professors, and friends.
When he came home
He brought light into the house.
His gray-haired uncle Jacob
Sometimes wondered, good-naturedly,
Where all the aimless subjects would lead,
And teased him, calling him a "dreamer."
But the old grandfather understood
The grandson better than Jacob did. With love
And respect, he listened and watched him.
After David came back home,
The relatives got together
For a discussion about his goals.
Uncle Jake said: This young man should
Get all that nonsense out of his head,
And all the dreams he has had till now,
Roll up his sleeves, and start
To work in our place. His head is good.
How long can a person play?
The doctor Willard thought it best
To buy the offspring a pharmacy.
He, the doctor, had confidence in its success.
The household was astounded
When David, quiet, sure, sedate,
Spoke out firmly: He would not
Accept Uncle Jacob's suggestion,
Nor would he listen to Uncle Willard's advice.
Indeed, he had something else in mind.
He has decided
To devote himself to agriculture.
His mother became like a stone.
She had other dreams for her son.
And the same was true for Aunt Ethel.
Uncle Willard picked up his hat
And left the house without a "Good-bye."
Uncle Jacob, stupefied,
Soon started to smile.
The grandfather, Josh, seated on a rocking chair,
Put his old hand up to his ear
As if he couldn't believe what he had heard.
The pipe fell out from between his teeth,

He picked himself up, out of the chair,
A living question mark: "Ey?"
Only Aunt Vivian
Was happy with David's words:
She immediately put her arms around the youth,
Pressed him to her heart and kissed him.

From where did the inspiration come to this youth,
The son of generation upon generation of tradesmen
Who were distant from and strangers to the earth,
Removed from her essence and power and smell?
Could it be that it came instinctively,
Subconsciously, that he wanted
To revive his own strength with earth.
Could it be that it came from the simplicity
Of a proud, refreshing, energetic nature
Which set the young man against
Following in the footsteps of his fathers and grandfathers.
Or did the great thinkers
Exercise an influence over him
Which prevented his from adapting
To the easy, familiar life-styles?
Whatever, the youth succeeded.
Uncle Jacob said that they
Might have expected that from him.
He always knew that some crazy idea
Would come into the dreamer's head.
Only Vivian, and later, too, old Josh
Were steadfast as steel and iron.
When the old man wrote out a check
For the price of a good farm
He wrote it almost with pleasure.
He groaned, his hand trembled, he blew on the check.
But in his old lifeless eyes
Something shimmered, as though through tears.
The odor of earth intoxicated him,
He slapped his grandson on the back,
Winked to him with a sly smile,
Rubbed his hands with excitement:
"Oh, what good apples we'll eat."

But the good apples were a long time in coming.
They first had to endure times

149

Of pox and measles. It took
The strong spirited nature of the youth
To live through everything. During this time
He isolated himself from the world,
And had not time to look into a book.
He was busy with cows, chickens, and
With nursing the tobacco and the corn.
When the mothers complained
That Lizzy, Molly, or Reddy
(David's holsteins) were dearer to him than they were,
The son smiled, openly—unrestrained—
With flashing teeth and excited eyes.
When they got lonely and wanted to see him,
They had to search him out on the farm.
They came unexpectedly in the limousine,
Visited a bit, cleaned the house,
And brought a table full of goodies.
At first the women complained
And worried about his fine, tender hands
Which became hard, raw, red,
And prickly as a grater.
But later, looking at him closely,
And seeing how manly the youth became,
How power and energy seemed to sprout
From the elastic, muscular, tanned body
And the honest gentle face,
The mothers were happy,
Their faces radiant,
And like children they drew close to him.

But then, when things got tight,
David came down to the city.
The grandfather, Josh, already knew what it meant,
And immediately assumed a stern face,
Or, indeed, fell into a melancholy
From which it was hard to arouse him.
But the grandson brought him around,
And the following conversation took place:
Josh:
A guest, descended as if from heaven.
We'll have to set the table. Sam, where are you?
(He pretends to look for the black Sam,
And digs, as it were, into his pocket.)

David: (With a smile)
Thank you. Don't trouble yourself, Grandfather.
Josh:
But still—oh yes, incidentally, how come
He indulges and tears himself away from the farm?
The cows will cry their eyes out there,
And who will take them for a walk today?
David:
(Bursting out with ringing, loud laughter
So that the grandfather must join
With hoarse, elderly gasps.)
It happens sometimes—better it shouldn't.

Here David becomes serious and starts to talk
As if to an older, loyal, good friend:
Thus and thus, so and so—
Here we need a stall, here we need something else,
It is absolutely necessary. The grandfather
Can see it for himself.

Josh: (Very melancholy)
So that means . . . ?
David: (Very sad)
                    A thousand dollars.
(The old man jumps up as if scalded,
Opens his mouth wide—a desolate field—
One yellow tooth here, another there,
Throws out his trembling hands
And groans imploringly): A thousand dollars!
David: (With an earnest, humble expression)
A thousand dollars.
Josh: (With a sly expression)
A small matter, only a thousand dollars?
And won't you take less?
David: (With his mind made up)
No.
Josh: (sedate)
And will you take more?
David:
Not more, either.
For now a thousand will be enough.
According to all the figures
A thousand dollars will be enough, enough.

Josh: (he talks now with entreaties)
It's not available. Who has so much cash?
David: (businesslike)
Well, grandfather could sign a note,
They'll give money on his signature.
Josh: (frightened)
A note?
And who will pay the interest on it?
David: (smiling)
Well, I will pay.
Josh: (almost crying)
Yes, with my money.

But later, when the business is finished,
And David kisses the grandfather's yellow hand,
The old man, already indifferent to money,
Gets up to accompany his grandson.
As he leans on David's strong arm,
His old, wrinkled face become animated,
And he is sorry that the boy is leaving.
He holds onto the lapels of David's coat,
And shakes a finger in his face,
Talking half earnestly, half playfully
Looking around to see that Jacob is not there:
He must not fall for a Gentile girl.
That is, actually, Vivian is
As dear to him as his own child,
But one in the family is enough, enough . . .
And David laughs and barely slips out
Of his grandfather's old, boney hands.

D. The Day

*O*h! the bright wonderful days
Of our rich, golden autumn!
It is really not autumn, but summer,
A second summer, bright, golden, red,
Mixed with dark green, bronze, copper,
And vermillion, and the deep blue of the sky.

These are days like wonderful dreams
With much fullness, warmth, and plenty.

The earth spreads out and lets itself go gently,
Tired from its heavy overflow,
Giving off heat
With ripe, full laziness, like a satisfied mother
Who has just nursed her child.
The child is full, raises its head,
And milk still drips from the full breasts.

Warm breezes blow.
The clear moving air is
Like old fragrant wine.
With every breeze, new fragrances
Intoxicate the brain.

Even richer than the day is the morning
When the fiery rim of the sun
Floats out of the blue soft darkness,
And everything takes on an unreal appearance,
Becomes an unknown world
Of unfamiliar, airy colors,
And peculiar, mysterious forms.
The gray trees emerge,
Suddenly their heads are in flames,
The flame slips down lower,
And a tree burns, a carnival of colors,
Leaves, bright red,
Yellow, and deep green,
Everything covered
With dew, the silver-gray breath of night.
The dew runs, flows, evaporates,
And the tree burns with many colors.

Later, light is added to the blue background
And, great God, what a wonder for the eye:
Curled heads of cabbage, tightly leaved,
Juicy fresh, heavy, stiff, and moist,
Long, blackish-green watermelons
With long, yellow spots on their bellies,
Wrapped in nets of yellow leaves.
Large heavy, red tomatoes,
Split from too much juice,
Drag down their plants
And lie on the earth, their mother.

Everywhere the grapevines, full and heavy,
Pour down from the fences
In heavy, overflowing, thick bunches,
Covered with gray dew.
The fever of wine climbs
And creeps everywhere, fills the air
With its sharp, sweet, hot smell.
And birds, birds, birds everywhere,
Red breasts and blue wings,
Black legs and red legs,
Each singing a different song
And warbling and twittering in its own way.

A man can live his life, busy
With his daily, enslaving work,
Carried away and dragged down by his worries,
And never even notice these wonders.
But it sometimes happened, that the same man sees
All of this from a new perspective. The familiar
Suddenly becomes new and fresh and unfamiliar,
An unknown world. The eye becomes pure,
It sees that which it had not seen.
And the man is astonished, excited, frightened.

On a certain day, old Josh
Arose at daybreak, as was his custom,
Grumbling to the old, black maid:
How come breakfast has no taste or flavor,
As usual. He lit his pipe
And quietly slipped out into the garden,
His old body bent.
He hobbled down the stairs,
Caught his breath with difficulty,
Sat down in the old rocking chair,
Raised his lifeless eyes,
And suddenly, the miracle occurred.

It was as if a thick skin
Was peeled off of his old eyes, and his look
Became clear, sharp, and bright.
His ears, which were dull,
Suddenly began to hear. Sounds
Trembled and vibrated in the thin air.

Stream after stream of air flowed,
And every stream unique:
Here is the smell of blessed wine,
And here the fragrance of cool winter apples,
The odor of sweet cool mint follows,
And the bitter sharp scent
Of dried, yellow tobacco.

The old man's nostrils twitch
Greedily seeking the currents of air.
The eyes, seeing, take in
The surrounding countryside. Everything
Stands open, wide, and uncovered:
Each pebble, blade of grass, bush and bloom,
Each fringe of the nearby curtains
On pink windows. It is amazing
How color mixes with sound
In one harmonious and clear outpouring.

The old man felt good, he did not think,
He only felt free, spontaneous.
And his heart beat as feverishly and fast
As a youth in love. He let himself go,
Abandoning himself to his feelings.
He let himself down to the rock bottom
Of emotion, and he felt the joy
And the passionate grief of dissolution.
Blissfully, he closed his tired eyes.

From now on tangible life
Became unreal, strange, unnecessary.
The black man quietly woke him from sleep:
The car is waiting in its usual place.
Josh motioned him away with his hand
Again surrendering himself to his feelings.
... There, somewhere, in the noisy city
Is the house which he built,
And merchandise, customers, notes, money ... for what?
He shrugs his old shoulders.
It is good here. Before his old eyes
A large, blinding sun shines.
He sees in front of him familiar faces,
Which became distant, strange, as if from another world.

As if through a wall,
Familiar, yet strange, voices come to him.
He feels himself carried through the air
Over distant abysses.
Time stops. The landscape, pink,
A deep void with a large disc
Of a fantastically large red sun.
And in the large red disc, someone
Walks with a pack on his back
Walks and walks and walks.
He musters all his strength
And smiles broadly, blissfully,
And even gestures with his yellow hand.
The pinkness remains. And in his head
Swim fantasies and pictures
Which assume wonderful shapes.
Fragments of Psalms entwine
With fragments of thoughts and feelings
Without beginning, without end.
A lullaby that small girls sing,
Recorded unconsciously
In the old man's mind, repeats itself:
"Rock me to sleep in my old Kentucky home,
And cover me with Dixie's blue sky...."
1921–1922

John

John

A.

*W*omen, whiskey, horses:
　　Kentucky stands by virtue of these three.
And John would defend this rule with his blood.
But then, John is young, tall, and strong,
A six-foot giant with muscles like ropes,
His tanned face perpetually laughing,
Blue eyes sparkling like a child's,
Brown hair curling rakishly.
Johnny laughs out loud
In the company of his buddies at the tavern.
Then the full glasses on the tables rise,
Move, shake, clink,
And the big belly of the bartender trembles.

Johnny, you should know, traces his lineage
To the first generation of pioneers
When Kentucky was still one big forest,
As entangled and overgrown, as it had been
When God at creation had released it from His hand.
In the untamed hills, Johnny's grandfathers
Cut the first trails, with ax and saw,
And always with a loaded gun at hand
In case the red devils
Attacked them. Stubbornly, man, woman and child

159

Fought for their scalps.
Johnny's grandmothers knew
How to handle a gun as well as the men did,
Shoot wild ducks, turkeys, and rabbits,
Set traps for the golden-red foxes,
Black skunks and soft brown mink.

Small wonder then that Johnny carries in his blood
The heat of unrestrained passion,
The speed and leap of the wild deer,
The eye of the eagle, and the hand of iron.
He did not inherit the constantly bitter eye,
Nor the closed, compressed lips
Of his great grandfathers,
Traits fixed by persistent battle.
Johnny's eyes sparkle clear and sure
And their blueness laughs; Johnny's lips
Always twitch with a good-natured smile
Revealing a mouth of sound white teeth.

His blood was restless.
While still a child in the Kentucky hills,
John read the forest like a book.
He dug "May apples" in the early spring
And ginseng roots which look like ginger,
Smoked the bees out of trees,
And brought home pots of honey.
He knew the place and the trees in which
The wild turkeys sleep.
He disappeared from the cabin
For days on end, in search of loot.
He knew where to get eggs,
Wild fowl, and where to catch fish.
Later, after the snow
Descended, soft, quiet, dependable,
Covering the ground with a white sheet,
The hills presented a new page for Johnny
From which he read every print and step
Of the fox, skunk, the wild rat and rabbit.
With a bloodhound's sharp, sensitive intuition
He smelled out the little animals
And knew where to hide traps.
In the evening Johnny arrived home

Loaded with booty, bringing into the house
The green forest flavor and the smell or snow
Mixed with that of the blood of stripped skins.

The youth quickly became
As tall and powerful as a tree.
He found a still in the mountains
Where "moonshine" was made.
One must say he forced
The sheriffs to work hard for their pay.
Nothing in the forest was hidden from Johnny,
He took lessons from the fox and skunk.
The still, stuck somewhere in a cliff,
Was so well hidden,
Naturally covered with shrubs and grass,
That it needed an eye like Johnny's
To discover it. In addition, one also needed
Johnny's courage and his steady handed
Skill with a gun.
Who but Johnny would risk a healthy head
For a sick bed? Johnny alone,
Behind a tree, could ward off ten,
And then slip out of their hands.
Thus, Johnny's reputation spread.
His name was known
From Kentucky to the hills of Tennessee.
And when he descended from the hills to the city,
Eyes laughing, hair long,
Johnny was already considered a hero.
People automatically made way for him.
If he happened to meet a sheriff he knew,
Johnny bowed and tipped his hat,
Smiled slyly, winking one blue eye.
The girls stole glances at John
And blushed, caressed by the blue fire.

Thus, Johnny's life proceeded
From hill into city, from city to the still,
From the still, in black, stormy nights,
Loaded with "moonshine," to Tennessee
Where Johnny already had his customers.
More than once, the youth
Took his life in his hands;

More than one bullet
Whizzed past Johnny's ear.
His body carried ample evidence
Of those nights, when he rode like the wind,
As if he and his horse were one.
But when one is young, one laughs off everything.
And Johnny laughed, as a man laughs
Who has a well of red life
Which turbulently storms, and seethes, and boils.
When he came back into the city
Not even knowing how much money he had,
His excitement simmered down
Only when his pockets were empty.
Because to Johnny money was cheap—
He could always get more.
And if, by chance, he picked a quarrel,
Started a fight in the bar
And beat a Negro to a pulp,
He was then led into court.
The judge, a clever, seasoned elder,
With young gray eyes behind glasses,
Would look him over, and smiling would order
A bed to be made up for the youth for the next seven days.
His buddies would come every day
To visit him, bringing with them
Flat, red flasks,
And pockets full of cigarettes and fruit.
Johnny, sleeping it off
And snoring in the lair, like the bear in the forest,
Gained weight. And after seven days,
Back to the still in the wilds.

B.

*T*he city lured Johnny:
   The tumult and commotion enticed him,
The movies bewitched him
And like a child stands in front of a curious toy
So did he sit enchanted in front of the screen.
Then came his time for love.
Of course, John wandered in the street
With eyes wide open, excited,

Heart beating and breath bated,
Drunk on women's hot glances.
The rustle of a woman's dress aroused him.
Hips in tightly cut dresses,
Lovely, slender, shapely legs in silk
Lit fires in his blood.
John became so familiar in the dance hall
That no dance started without him.
The girls clustered around him
Like bees around honey: it was
A glorious time for John.
The brass trumpet kept time for him,
And the drum beat to the rhythm of his blood,
No one was his equal,
And no one moved like him
In familiar convoluting Negro dances,
The belly-dance and the hootchy-kootchy.
The ground burned under his feet
And girls swung like angels,
And Johnny's heart and blood burned
Hot with desire.

John was thrilled by all this.
Every nerve and drop of blood
Soaked up the red stream of life.
He devoted his days to tumult
And his nights to love. It seemed as if
The youth flew on wings, walked bouncing,
His broad chest thrust out, his head thrown back,
A short, smoking pipe in the corner of his mouth,
His strong limbs clearly outlined
Under a blue shirt and brown velvet trousers.

That roses have thorns is an old maxim,
And Johnny learned the rule on his own hide.
More than once Johnny was surprised
In little side streets of the city,
With sticks, rods of iron, stones,
In short, with whatever can break bones.
He was worked over properly.
More than once the ambulance sounded for him
And Johnny should have thanked God
That he escaped with his life.

These were husbands and bridegroom lovers
Who gave Johnny to understand
That he should not steal into other's gardens.
For a week or two Johnny would go around decorated
With red biles like eggs under his eyes,
Or a black sling around his neck
In which his arm rested.
But John accepted the wounds gladly
And carried no enmity on their account.
It was all part of the game,
When ones take honey from the bee,
One can't begrudge her an angry sting.
Johnny had yet another passion
Which might outweigh the rest: horses.
Not for nothing does Kentucky pride itself
On its wonderfully strong horses.
The blue grass of the broad plains
Is soft, fragrant, and succulent.
Water flows in cool clear streams.
Small wonder that the horse prances, gambols, thrives.
It gets washed and brushed,
Combed and cared for like a precious jewel,
Its tail plaited into black or blond braids.
When the horse is taken out of its stall for air,
The ground rocks under its feet.
Not too tall and not too short, broad breast,
Small belly, elongated head,
Large soft eyes, brown and clever,
Its fine ears trembling nervously,
Its legs graceful, thin, and muscular.
Under its gleaming coat
Every nerve quivers.

C.

*A*nd so from the dance hall to the stall
John lived his stormy life.
Too short the day, too short the night.
He really lived. He couldn't understand
How it came to pass that he felt
Closer to Margaret, more at home with her,
Than with any other girl.

Margaret was really beautiful:
Slender, blond, with soft, round limbs,
Mild, gray, mischievous eyes
Under shining, golden brows.
When she appeared with him in the street
In her high red-laced boots
Which touched the hem of her white dress,
Blue bows around her thin neck,
A white picture hat on her head
From which curls peek,
Johnny's heart filled with joy,
Men turned their heads
To look at the petite Margaret
Who swayed gracefully like a kitten
At the side of tall, broad John.

Margaret loved this John
With every bone of her tender shapely body.
The youth stole into her heart
And her family could not drive him out,
Neither could whips nor fists.
The truth is
That the family was right:
True, John is a fine boy,
A spirited youth, who is handy with everything.
But what good is that, if he is a devil
Who plays with whatever women are around,
And will continue to play till his death.
Today he is here, tomorrow he is there.
Who can catch the wind in the field?
For days on end, Margaret's young brothers
Sang a song on this theme
Which began with the words:
        "Johnny's here and Johnny's there,
        Johnny is everywhere."
But argue today, argue tomorrow, the girl
Refused to listen—and that's the end.
They argued so long
They got sick of it,
Spit and threw up their hands.
Let the girl worry her own head,
No good will come of it.

Margaret had her way:
With great joy and happiness, she led
John to the church. It was hard
To do this, because Johnny
Felt very uncomfortable in the church,
He had never poked his nose in there,
And had avoided it
As the devil avoids the smell of incense.
But this time no tricks came to his aid.
To spite all the women
Who threw their work aside
And came to look at the fine pair approaching,
Johnny arrived on time,
Took the vows as he was supposed to,
And led Margaret home,
A fine, young, well-behaved master.

It is necessary to be just to Johnny,
And say that he is a good husband.
Because, in fact, he is by nature good
And Margaret is devoted and loyal to him.
The youth gave up his hills
And took a job like everyone else.
They were not worried about a living,
There was plenty to sustain them:
Their cottage outside the city
Is immersed in a sea of vegetables in the summer,
Everything a household needs.
The cow gives milk, the hens, eggs,
And when they kill the pig—he gives meat.
And when John wakes at dawn,
Margaret has been up for hours.
The table is set, the coffee perks in the pot
And the smell of hot biscuits makes his mouth water.
Margaret, in a white apron,
Cleans the house, or takes care of the yard
And feeds the cows and fowl.
When John comes home in the evening
The house is tidy, all the corners clean.
The food smells good, and Margaret, dressed up,
Has, as always, a sweet smile.
True, it happens that the youth often gets lost,
Disappears for a whole night, is nowhere,

Shows up again at the break of day,
Often comes back with torn clothes,
Bruised, ragged, a pity to see.
Well, what can one do? Margaret washes him
Helps him undress, and puts him to bed.
Later, when he quietly falls asleep
And smiles childishly in his dreams,
She cannot restrain a smile herself:
Well, really, how can one be angry with him?
It won't help. Whether she wants it or not,
Johnny must "sow his wild oats."
When all is said, John is completely hers.
He will run a little, play a little, and that's all.
Why turn her home into hell?

Margaret bore a son,
And he was given the name John,
John junior.
Little John grew
Opened wide his blue eyes,
Clapped his little soft hands,
And laughed showing dimples in his face.
John became more of a homebody,
And disappeared less often.
His buddies mocked him,
Regretting what can happen to a man like John.
John smiled a guilty smile.
But how could he help himself?
Margaret is dear and sweet—and blossoms,
And John junior grows and laughs.
When John senior comes into the house in the evening
His heart does not yearn for any other place.
In short, John is a different person.
The family came to the conclusion
That Margaret did not do so badly
By not being afraid of the youth.
Her brothers slap him on the back,
And come more frequently to visit.
Comfortable, they sit on the porch
In the warm, rose-colored dusk;
They joke, and tell each other news.
Blue smoke curls thickly
Rising from fragrant pipes.

D.

*T*here is in Kentucky an old custom:
　　At summer's end, when the fields are cut,
And the trees bend with the weight
Of heavy, succulent, ripe fruit,
A celebration takes place in the county seat.
On a lawn outside the city
Canvas booths are set up
Where the good and plenty of wood and field
Are exhibited for people to admire:
The finest products of the fruit trees,
The finest vegetables from gardens,
The finest handwork in wool and linen
Embroidered by women in the long winter nights,
In stormy nights by a kerosene lamp,
In a far flung corner of the hills.
The most beautiful milking cows,
The fattest, most playful sheep and calves,
And, above all, the young, restless horses.
From one hill of Kentucky to the other
The folk in a holiday mood gather
For the celebration, packing the big field
Which smells of flowers, apples, and of earth,
With odors of the stall and green tobacco.
Over it all hangs a blue sky,
A calm, peaceful, end-of-summer sky,
And the strains of an orchestra are heard.
Every year, the holiday is celebrated
For seven whole, long, bright days.

Have you seen the annual fair
In one of the fine Southern towns?
The market is fully and very congested.
The paths overflow with goods from the field,
Vegetables which smell and sparkle with freshness,
Apples, pears, plums, red melons
With large, heavy, transparent seeds.
Sheep bleat, pigs squeal,
Horses whinny, and donkeys plod along,
Roosters crow, geese scream.
The hill people come down to the fair,
Black and red beards
On their red, tanned faces,

And colored kerchiefs around their necks.
A blind beggar plays a tearful song,
And small Black children spin in a dance
Quickly, nimbly swinging their black limbs.
The whites of their eyes sparkle
Like sweet cream from out of a black earthenware crock.
Later, when the flaming sun sets,
The field becomes spacious, a play in red.
Suddenly a Black minister jumps
Up onto a flat wagon, starts singing,
A circle gathering round him.
The Negro shakes and throws himself around in ecstasy
And strikes his fat belly and his chest,
His teeth flash and his eyes stare,
And everyone picks up his song,
A holy song well known from church.
And the red, dying sun plays
On faces carved of copper and cast iron.

When the holiday came to the city,
John threw all his work aside.
Margaret took a basket of food.
And John junior, dressed in white,
His face flushed, his eyes large,
Clapped his hands and sang and chattered loudly
As his father carried him through the large crowd.
The drums beat and the brass played along,
And Johnny's feet were ready for dancing.

Johnny spends with an open hand.
He doesn't miss a game, not a single booth.
He spins with little Johnny
On the carved horses of the carousel,
And on the high swinging cradles,
Flies on the small, roller coaster,
Which plunges down a high hill.
When evening comes, little John
Is loaded with toys,
Red, blue, green balloons,
Little boxes of candy, little baskets of fruit,
Little flutes, whistles, and horses.

One day the following occurred:
Little John began to feel sick,

From the strain and heat,
Too many sweets and too much spinning.
His cheeks were burning,
His little golden head swayed helplessly,
His bright eyes, half-closed,
Did not see the toys.
It was hard for Margaret to leave
And go home in the middle of such an important day.
But what can one do when a child is sick?
Johnny put her into a car
And he himself remained at the fair.

The races were in full swing.
In the large ring spread
With yellow sparkling sand, the track
Lay bright and sunny.
Six or seven horses impatiently
And restlessly paw the ground with their hoofs,
Their limbs quivering nervously.
A rope, drawn across the breadth of the track,
Reaching up to the horses' noses
Drops down to the ground
As soon as a flag is lowered.
One second, the horses hold back, nervously,
But in the same wink of the eye, a push forward,
A stretching out of all the stiff limbs
And the wide track disappears under them.
Now they fly together as if in one lump,
Breast to breast, head to head, inseparable.
Now one horse breaks away,
And after him another, and the rider's head and body
Are stretched out and leaning towards the far horse.
The crowd on the rows of benches in the casino
Come out of their dead silence,
Their breath comes back, faces flame,
The white handkerchiefs wave overhead
And a loud, jubilant cry rises.
Johnny, it seems, does not stay in one place,
But glides with the flying horses
His eyes eager, hands spread out.
He is on fire together with the large crowd.

In the meantime, the sun sets in the west.
The green field is dipped in red,

And red covers the white canvas booths
And the distant green treetops.
The grass becomes darker, thicker, bluer,
Girls laugh out loud
And boys try to sing and frolic at the same time.
The casino is bathed in light,
And the brass band plays.
The dance hall is packed with young couples,
And now John displays his talent.
The girls keep changing,
Flushed and tired, they drop out,
But he continues dancing,
Intoxicated in the gliding crowd,
His eyes half closed, his mouth closed.
At his chest, a yielding body
Clings to him trembling.

It was very late
When he finally left the dancehall,
A tired, breathless girl at his side,
The fresh cool night engulfed
The soft, black, fragrant earth.
White figures crouched in the field
And couples stretched themselves out on the grass,
Girls quietly surrendering
To black shadows.
Johnny did not know how
He happened to wander into the soft field,
With a girl, in the black night.
Actually, Johnny did not intend any harm.
The black summer night seized him,
Blinded him, excited him with its lust.
The fragrant earth which oozes moisture
Set fire to his volatile blood.
The girl, Violet, now child, now woman,
With her fifteen years of young life,
Offered her fresh lips
And excited him with her glowing eyes.
A child of the South ripens early,
Has hot blood, small firm breasts.
John felt her breath on his neck,
Felt the soft, trembling throb
Of her fresh, fragrant body.
Passionately, he pressed the small girl

Into his muscular, strong arms.
Crickets chirped in the night,
Frogs croaked from the swamps.
And a black, smoldering sky
Bent itself over the Kentucky field.

E.

*B*ut the next morning, when John went to work
Death met him.
                              The girl's father
Posted between bushes on the road
Waited with an old gun
And pumped five bullets into him.
And before he had time to say "Jesus"
The youth was lying on the ground,
Like a young, strong oak
Struck down by angry lightning.
In front of his not yet dead eye, swam
The tops of the trees at the side of the road,
And pieces of blue, flowing sky.
The large, round sun
Just risen from the east
Lay red in front of him on the green grass.
And for a while his ear reverberated
With distant muffled thunder.

When he was lying in the coffin
Clean, and religious, in his best suit,
Blond hair curled in large rings,
His face soft and pale as if sleeping,
Margaret, young and wan,
Bent over him,
Caressing the shining soft hair,
The pale forehead, whispering quietly
For hours on end, murmuring in his ear:
"My hero, my child, my poor child, my angel,
Sleep peacefully, sleep in your young grave,
John junior will grow up like you,
And will revenge your spilled blood.
My hero, my child, my sweet husband, my angel."
John junior clung to her.

172

Frightened, looking at his pale father,
Who lay smiling quietly as if asleep.

Birds sang in the orchard
And a hot sun looked into the room.
It smelled of incense,
Of full blown flowers,
Of fields, and of a new day.

Joe

Joe

A. A Greenhorn Comes

*W*hen a greenhorn turns up
    And comes to an uncle or a brother,
He is allowed first to rest.
The boiling kettle of water sings and spurts,
The kitchen smells of hot yellow *hallah*
And home made spiced honey cake.
Early in the morning the *shoykhet* kills some fowl,
Livers and fat are fried.
The woman brings all sorts of good things to the table:
Home-brewed mead and wine,
And all sorts of preserves from the cellar.
It is impossible to chase the children from the house.
They poke their fingers in the preserves,
Pinch off bits of honey cake to dip in the brandy,
Run errands—are back in a flash.
Their eyes sparkle eagerly, like the eyes of little wolves.
After the heavy rich meal, the men smoke
Thick, fragrant cigars.
The rockers creak heavily in the room,
The air is hot and soporific, the smoke
Circles and wraps around the faces
Of grandfathers and grandmothers on the walls.

Having slept, having received the regards
From relatives, strangers from the whole world,
The guest is shown around by the host
To see how people live in this new world.
First he shows him his own estate,
His house, barn, prize cow, and chickens,
Tells him the whole story of how
He worked himself up.
The guest swallows curious words
Like "mortgage, note, junk, and second-hand."
He gapes and makes believe that he understands,
Blinks with pitying eyes,
Helplessly throwing up his hands
Which stick out from his new "second-hand."
Later, they take him into the broad street.
They stop at each shop window,
And look over the fine things.
When the uncle sees a familiar Gentile
He breaks into a warm, friendly smile,
And greets him in English.
The "greenhorn" stands amazed, looks at their mouths,
And thirstily tries to drink in every word.
If an automobile appears on the street,
The uncle shows his knowledge on the spot. He calls out
The name and the price of the racer
As if the greenhorn were ready to buy;
He claps him expansively on the back:
Doesn't matter. You'll become Americanized and you'll buy.

On the third day of the guest's arrival,
After he has learned
To count to one hundred on his fingers,
The two men retire to a quiet room,
And the guest is told: "Say, Jack or Joe,
It's time to think about business."
And Jack or Joe perks up his ears,
And receives an account of the many hardships
Which the uncle or the brother endured:
The story of how they starved,
How they journeyed with the pack,
And how they kept their noses to the grindstone.
And Jack, or Joe, sits guiltily,

His cigar limp in his hand,
Lips curled in an aimless smile.

On the morrow, he is led into a store.
They prepare a large pack and a long list:
Sheets, tableclothes, towels,
Women's dresses, hairpins, combs,
Colored beads and thick glasses.
They teach the greenhorn the prices,
How to quickly unpack and repack,
They wish him luck and fortune,
And a start on the right foot. They say thus:
"It'll work out. It'll be all right. It has to.
When you see a door, knock. It'll open.
Just don't be a greenhorn. Sell.
Well, well. You'll learn the art.
A man is not a bear. Well, good luck."
Thus Jack, or Joe, sets out,
With his heavy new business on his back
Across the hills and dales of Kentucky.

B. Business

*T*he old trails run far and wide,
   And it is far from one farm to the other.
Yusl, or Joe, walks with his back bent,
The pack seems heavy, like a mountain,
A tremendous harsh mountain
Growing on his back. And it presses on him.
In the summer, the heat burns and roasts him alive,
And bores into him like red-hot spears.
In the winter, the frost is piercing and the wind cutting,
The cold snow lashes and blinds the eyes.
He sees a door—knocks—it is opened.
But how does one do business,
When there is no common speech?
And so, great sorrow speaks mutely,
In the loneliness of the teary eyes,
The deep creases around the pale lips,
The lament of the red, swollen hands.
If he happens on a farm at lunchtime

When the household sits around the table,
Engrossed in pork and brown potatoes,
Yusl is invited to eat at the table.
He somehow gets out of it:
He merely wants to rest from the weary way
And straighten out his cramped bones.
A group of children with flaxen heads and watery eyes
Cluster around him.
They touch and smell the cold pack
Which strayed here from the distant world.
Later, when the table is cleared,
And the farmer, with a pipe, rocks in the rocking chair.
They then remember that Jim needs boots,
The little girl needs socks and gloves.
The pack suddenly appears on the table.
They search, and feel, and try on.
The children wear the new things immediately
And feel more at east with Yusl;
They hang on to his coat
And take delight in his curious speech.

When the transaction is finished,
And he's caught his breath, warmed his body,
Yusl remembers that he is hungry.
He drags out of the pack a loaf of bread,
Cuts and salts an onion, and eats.
The Gentile shrugs his shoulders and thinks:
What a funny guy. He doesn't like hot biscuits
Baked in the best lard,
He wants no pork or potatoes,
But here he sits and swallows frozen bread,
Stale, dried out bread with onions and salt.
The farmer sits and wonders, and looks at him
Through the newly bought glasses
Until something occurs to him.
So he says to Yusl: "What! A Catholic Jew?"
And Yusl shakes his head yes.

Later, when Yusl walks again with his pack,
He feels more at ease. The path is covered in white,
The sky friendly, the wind caressing.
He continues on the old white trail

And recites Psalms by heart,
With the old *Rosh Hashana* melody
Which he brought with him from the old country.

Month after month run by,
And with them the business-on-the-move grows,
As Joe catches on to the language
And "Jewish Joe" becomes known.
Even the dogs know him
And are friendly. They wag their tails for him.
When the children of some distant farm
See him coming from afar,
They are as delighted with him as with a father.
Now, he no longer drags a pack.
It lies comfortably in a wagon,
And Joe drives a horse and enjoys it.
His territory grows, and with it his trade.
He buys out everything which comes his way:
A calf, a bale of wool, a bundle of flax,
A pot of honey, a hide, and furs.
And Friday, when he comes into the city,
The little wagon is full to the brim.
The horse smells the air of the uncle's barn,
The children hang on to him like bees,
The aunt serves fresh fish,
The uncle is very cheerful and smiles,
And repeats every week the same thing:
"Aha! I said right away that it'll be all right."

C. The Calamity

*O*nce, on a hot summer's day,
Joe dragged himself to a distant farm in the hills.
It was hot and quiet as death,
The July sun beat overhead,
Shooting sparks on the red roof
And baking the hard black ground.
The flowers around the house wilt,
Bending their heads sadly, about to faint.
The hens creep into the shadows,

Pigs dig around wells,
And Nigger, the shaggy black dog,
Abandons his body to the flies,
Stretches himself out, his long tongue panting.
The small windows of the farmhouse
Are wide open.
Before Joe has time to water
His tired horse, the girl Suzy
Suddenly springs up in front of him like a shadow:
Red, shapeless, fat,
Her face heavy, dull, and motionless,
Her watery eyes reflect
The fear of a dog trembling at the whip.
And before he knows it, she falls to the ground,
Tightly grabbing him around the knees,
Kissing his rough, red hands,
Banging her head on the hard ground
And on his dusty heavy shoes,
Talking, crying, talking, crossing herself,
And calling on Jesus for help.
The youth immediately sees his calamity.
His knees tremble as if in fever,
And big round drops of sweat
Appear on his pale face.
He stammers, his tongue thick,
Tries to lift the girl from the ground,
But she stubbornly clings to the earth
As if she craved that it
Open a mouth and swallow her.

When the red apples started to fall
From the trees onto the green grass,
When the green tobacco leaves started
To yellow, and crumble,
Suzy could no longer hide her condition.
The mother pinched and hit,
The father stamped and hit,
The brothers hit with whips
Screaming filled the air.
The dog jumped around like a lion
Howling insanely,
Madly throwing himself against the whips,
Tearing and pulling at the coats.

182

The girl howled like a wild animal,
But did not defend herself, she lay demolished.
When they finally forced from her
The name of the father-to-be
The old farmer spit,
Jerking his hands away as if burned.
Her mother was turned to stone,
The brothers, who had rested their whips,
Started on her again with even more zeal.

When the initial tumult settled down,
The family sat around the table
To have a bit to eat. The old woman
Padded around the kitchen, and soon
Odors filled the house,
The smell of biscuits cooking
In rich lard, and hot coffee
Perking and gurgling in the pot.
The group became quiet, crossed themselves,
Wiped the sweat from their faces with their sleeves,
And greedily ate
While from the far corner, came
The agitated groaning of the girl
And the rumbling of the dog who snuggled
And nestled against her. The dog scowled
At them with moist, glistening eyes,
Wagging his long, hairy, black tail,
Licking himself with his reddish tongue,
And waiting to be invited
To the table. Meanwhile, the smell of
Strong, smoking pipes
Filled the house. The conversation
Started up anew,
But this time quieter, more restrained.
The youngest of the sons, indeed a fiery one,
Again, eagerly grabbed his whip
Ready to start work again.
But this time, the old man did not permit him.
He restrained his son
Pushed him back in his chair.
It's no trick, he said, to kill the girl.
What's done is done. However,

He would sooner have expected any disaster
But that his daughter should play such a trick.
And look at whom that bitch
Found to sniff around.
It'll be, said he, a fine pair, indeed:
A dummy and a devil. But it's done,
Just as she made her bed,
So will she sleep. Walt, the youngest son,
Stormed and stamped with outrage.
He kept on arguing that he would
Shoot that dirty "sheeney" like a dog.
For Walt, the match did not sit right
Because he, himself, was on the verge of a match,
And he was afraid, lest the new pedigree
Should harm his chances. So they
Had to argue and convince the youth
That there is no other way out of this misery.
They were trapped, that's all. They must
Wait for the Jew to arrive
And get rid of the mess, make an end of it.
But just between themselves, it is not so bad.
The girl didn't deserve better anyway,
A dummy of a girl, a lump of meat with two eyes.
The Jew seems to be a quiet man
And, like all Jews, he is loaded with money.
And besides, it's beyond help, it's done,
Signed, sealed, and delivered.
                              But Joe, as if in spite,
Stopped showing up there,
Disappeared, was nowhere.
The family watched in vain.
They lay in wait at all the paths,
Suzy wore her eyes out watching.
No sign of the Jew or of his horse.
They grew impatient with the long wait
And, one fine Sunday,
The menfolk gathered
And went to the city.

D. In-Laws

*I*t was a sunny afternoon,
  A day of rest, when the Southern city becomes

Sleepy after the rich noon meal.
The world lives through the Indian summer
With its flaming red leaves,
And fluttering white spider webs.
The small gardens around the houses are yellow,
The tomatoes glow red
And bend their bushes to the earth.
A warm wind blows and flutters
The large snowballs which have turned pink.
Everywhere, over everything, is
The charm and peacefulness of quiet summer,
Of blue sky and sun.

Sabbath-Sunday peace was
In Joe's uncle's house,
The green blinds pulled down
So that it was half dim and half light.
When the breeze frolicked, and pushed aside
A blind from the window, a golden strip,
Of sun gilded the opposite wall.
On the red flowered wallpaper
Hung in large gilt frames
Grandmothers in kerchiefs and wigs,
And grandfathers with skullcaps and beards.
Baron Hirsch and Jacob Schiff
Felt quite at home in this company.
The only one who scowled
Was Kerinsky in his fur hat,
Because he, Kerinsky, was hung
Just under the hanging clock,
And each time the black pendulum
Swung past his face, he
Scowled in the shadows. Besides all these,
There was a big crowd of "movie-stars"
On small cards assaulting the wall
As if thick, many colored locusts
Crept upon it. It was quiet.
The uncle was sitting in the rocking chair,
Sprawled out in his shirt sleeves and trousers,
Relaxed, his glasses on his forehead,
Wearing a skullcap, looking into
The papers, humming, at the same time
A melody from the Rosh Hashana service,
And cooling himself off with strong, hot tea.

Joe, in a heavy troubled sleep,
Thrashed on an old couch
In a corner of the room.
His face, pinched and flushed,
Nervous, restless, twitched
Piteously and quietly.
                              And into the quietness,
Suddenly, came from the street
The hard tramp of heavy boots,
And the anger of stubborn voices.
Through the open door four Gentiles
Like giants appeared, sun-burned,
With red faces and red necks.
The old man in front, with the gray beard,
And behind him, fuming, hot sons,
All with gleaming guns in hand.
The uncle, amazed, looked them over,
And then smiled, as if to ask:
"These lords come to pawn their guns?"
But he looked into their gray eyes,
Which were eager, sharp, and murderous.
He noticed how Joe hastily jumped up,
Then remained sitting, neither dead nor alive.
So the uncle, concluding that something was not right,
Rose from his chair,
Took two or three steps towards them,
Stopped, and with questioning fingers
And a feigned smile, asked the guests
Where they were going hunting in the middle of summer.
And now Walt sputtered out ferociously:
"We really are going hunting. Correct.
We are chasing a two-footed rabbit,
And if we are not mistaken, we will
Find the rabbit here in this house."
The old farmer found his voice.
He winked at Walt to be quiet,
Deliberately sat down at the table,
Took off the wide straw hat,
Slowly filled his pipe with tobacco,
Lit it, started blowing smoke puffs.
Only then he spoke to the pale uncle:
"Now neighbor, pull up a chair; we'll talk."
Meanwhile, he kept an eye on Joe,
Shrewdly winked at him, as if just spying him:

"Hey, Joe," he says, "long time no see,
Probably got so rich it doesn't befit him
To come into our parts.
The old lady is looking her eyes out for him,
And Suzy is dying to see him sometime.
He wouldn't recognize Suzy anymore.
She got fat and round like a barrel.
A pity Joe doesn't show up,
He could bet his bottom dollar that he would be
A most welcome guest in our house.
An important guest."
                              Upstairs, in the meantime,
The aunt woke from sleep, came down,
Her face flushed, but refreshed.
A look here, a look there, a word—
For the aunt a long story was not needed.
First, she became like a pillar of salt,
She couldn't even catch her breath.
Later, when she caught the drift of the conversation,
She started to yell:
A disaster happened, a curse from God,
An uncontrolled fire is in her house.
Her heart had told her, there was something
Wrong with the youth;
For the past few months he was walking around
Like a sleepwalker.
And she had taken care of this snake,
Who now puts a curse on them.
It's come to this. Good God!
These are, it seems, the in-laws.
The youth should have warned her
That he expected such guests.
She would have prepared some refreshments,
Would have cleaned house, washed the cats.
It's no trifling thing, such in-laws.
A pity, the brother-in-law Chaim Ber
Was not destined to see such joy.
We'll have to call him from the grave.
Yusl sat as if on fire.
The uncle, pale as whitewash,
Chewed on the point of his beard.

The blood was seething in the three brothers.
The color of blood was in their eyes.

187

The only one who remained quiet,
Feeling entirely at ease in the tumult,
Was the old man with his pipe.
He winked devilishly with shrewd eyes,
And blew clouds of smoke to the ceiling.
Nodding his head all the time,
He let the woman rant and rave.
In short, the aunt asks him, what does he want?
He wants, he says, nothing. But his daughter,
His daughter Suzy wants her man.
She has, he says, a claim on him,
And besides the claim, she has, as one can see,
Three good brothers.
If he had known before
That the stale fish would have to be begged,
He wouldn't have gotten mixed up in the business,
He would have just left it to his sons.
Well, neighbor, he says to the pale uncle,
Good luck, let's shake hands.
I like your wife, she has a mouth on her.
Joe'll come with us, the girl is lonely.
He has no time to play the future father-in-law,
He'll leave that for another time,
The tobacco in the fields waits for him.
And early tomorrow, they'll go
To the court and make an end to the business.
A little later when the in-laws
Left the house with Joe,
Bereavement spread into every corner.
The uncle wiped his teary glasses,
The aunt sobbed out loud.
In the house, the strong tobacco still smelled,
A remembrance of the just departed father-in-law.
Baron Hirsch and Jacob Schiff
Looked indifferently down from the wall,
And only Kerinsky was angry:
The world is not a wanton world, my young man.

E. Jew and Gentile

Severe, cutting north winds
Started blowing in the hills.

The last thin leaves of the trees
Dispersed in the valleys.
One morning, arising from sleep,
Joe saw a white world in front of him,
A white world, with white hills and trees,
White barns and a white well.
In the air, everything whirled and mixed;
The snow both fell and flew.
And then a long winter set in,
And day and night interchanged
Like in a long, indifferent dream,
Where sun and stars and moon alike
Scarcely illuminate a cloudy gray sky.

Life dragged on monotonously,
Grayness seemed to press into the very bones
And kill their last red drop of blood.
The men awoke at the crowing of the cock
And disappeared till evening in the hills.
"There he goes; Esau on the hunt," thought Joe
He retired into the deepest corner,
And wiled away the day, quiet, preoccupied.
The women worked quietly, unceasingly,
Like oxen in the harness: cleaned the barn,
Chopped the hard ice around the well,
Carried water for the cows and pigs,
Milked the cows, baked the bread,
And spun on the spinning wheel till late at night.
But Joe's hands were idle,
Every limb made of lead.
It was as if he carried
A stranger's head on his shoulders.
The old man merely shook his head:
What a carcass he had caught hold of,
A fine worker he had bargained for.
At first he had tried to cheer him up,
And take him along to the woods,
But he soon threw up his hands.
The two older sons ridiculed Joe,
Scowling at him wherever he was.
But Walt, the youngest, kept quiet,
Quiet as a cat, his lips pressed shut.
Hatred for the Jew burned in him,

Sometimes spilling out of his gray shrewd eyes
In a red murderous glance.
The only one who sympathized with Joe
Was his Gentile woman, his Suzy.
She served him his bread and potatoes,
His bit of milk, (pork sickened him) and
Quietly sidled up to him
As a dog sidles up to its master.
And then it was so quiet
That the quietness grated in their ears.

One day the profound stillness broke,
Like an ice-bound river bursts.
The mute gravid Gentile, his Suzy,
Suddenly stopped working.
She went to bed in the middle of the day
And fell into such a fit of screaming
That the ceiling overhead trembled.
The old woman worked around her daughter,
And Joe, as if in a dream, helped,
Kept the fire going with fresh wood,
Dragged pails of water from the well,
Kept warming the ice water.
And when the first cry of the newborn child
Trembled in the dim house,
His heart started fluttering
And silent tears rolled
Down his pale sunken cheeks.
The infant son was
A red, crying, wrinkled face,
Both hatefully foreign and pitifully close.

Later, spring arrived in the land.
First, the ice and snow melted
And streams rushed from the hills;
The air smelled of fresh earth
With rich, black soil and green trees.
The sun rose earlier each day,
Birds flew from everywhere
And spread, singing, nesting every place:
In the cornices of the house, the stall, the barn.
With the full, quiet powers
Floating in the air,

Joe clearly sensed that if he wanted
To stay alive, he must work.
If not, he'll rot like a plow
Which is no longer used. The work
At first was hard. It was
Both clumsy and strange. But little by little
He got used to it,
And caught on to the new life.
He worked as if intoxicated by his labor,
Doggedly oblivious to everything else.
For the first time in his life
He knew security and peace.
The old man watched, amazed.
He couldn't get over it;
Even the sons stopped their ridicule.
The only one that didn't change
Was Walt. He hated Joe.
But nothing bothered Joe.
He never mixed into their business,
They were all foreign, distant, and removed.
He didn't even say a word when
The family started to chop out
The old fruit orchard around the house
Because tobacco plants paid more.
His blood seethed with anger.
From out of his distant childhood came
A familiar forgotten passage from the Bible:
"Do not spoil any fruit tree." But,
Powerless to utter the thought,
He remained silent. He got used to the child.
In the chubby face, short nose,
And thin, white hair,
He found charm. A faint feeling of pity
For his wife, his fat, downtrodden stranger, Suzy,
Came into his heart.

It was funny, that through time
He lost his yearning for
The world he left behind.
Only once or twice did he go to the city
To his uncle's house,
Bringing them presents of fresh cheese,
A basket of eggs and some greens.

But he felt peculiarly strange and uncomfortable.
The uncle was silent in his own way,
The aunt, understanding his feelings,
Tried to draw him out, to make him talk,
Winking to him, implying that the world is big
And with money . . .
                        But Joe didn't answer.
He quietly bid them goodbye.
In the street, near the shops,
Familiar storekeepers stopped him, talked;
Friendly, they invited him into the store,
But he answered with an odd smile.
He knew that behind his back
More than one off-color joke was told
About him, his Gentile wife, and family.
They invited him a bit out of curiosity,
A bit out of business. But he didn't care,
Having grown out of all of that.
Unbeknownst to himself,
With each passing day, he became more attached to the earth
As if he had roots growing in the soil.
Run away? No. To run to what, and where?
He loves every piece of earth,
The old barn, the plow, and the house.
Drag around again on the road with the pack?
For the first time,
He begins to understand
The sure and powerful tone of the old man
Who wakes up at dawn in summer,
Sprinkles cold water on his face, and
Sings from a full, strong chest
Of the first arrival of the pilgrims,
Their battle, their sorrow and victory,
And of the great security and peace
Of the old Kentucky home and old glory.

F. Dust

*W*hite winter came again.
        The cottage smelled of wet skins
Which were hung to dry,
And of the strong, bittersweet odor

192

Of raw greenish-yellow tobacco leaves.
The child now crawled around on the ground,
Pulling on his fat mother's dress,
Trying to stand on his father's boots,
Playing with the big black dog
And with the newborn calf which
Was taken into the house because of the cold.
On one such bright day
When snow and sunbeams blended together,
The men carted the tobacco into the city
On large flat wagons.
The wheels crunched on the snow,
The horses, fed and rested, trotted along.
The menfolk were cheerfully excited,
The old man puffing and counting
On his fingers, talked of the market,
And of last year's price and weight.
A greedy green flame burned
In his crafty sly eyes.
The sons figured how much money
The old man would divide among them this time,
And how they would enjoy spending it
In the tumultuous city. Only Joe
Sat quietly. For him, it was good
To sit thus in the blue day,
With closed eyes, dreaming of nothing,
Lulled by the trotting of the obedient horses.
The warehouses in the city
Are clogged with wagons and automobiles.
The excitement of a fair hangs in the air,
One meets old friends,
Never seen from one year to the next.
They inquire about neighbors,
Talk about the market and their earnings,
And money fever burns in every eye.
They move around the large, crowded market
Where the produce of three quarters of Kentucky's soil
Lay spread out for sale on wagons.
They feel each other's tobacco,
They smell, rub a tobacco leaf, chew.
Later, they go over to the stores
To pick out presents for wife and child.
They go in groups from one store to the next,

They pose, they feel, they look around, they bargain,
They spit brown tobacco juice on the ground,
While pale, fast-moving Jews
Talk their lungs out to the yokels,
A taste of bitter gall in their mouths.
But the yokels remain cold and crafty,
They have time, they'll come again.
Later, the men return to the market.
They watch the wagons, drink beer,
They sleep through
The nights sitting with a beer in a bar somewhere.
In the morning they go back to the shops
And the bargaining begins again.

When they counted the money,
The old man's hands were frozen
And the paper slid from them.
Every second he forgot where he was
And started counting again from the beginning.
The sons were impatient,
Eager to count the money themselves.
But the old man didn't budge;
He counted with feverish eyes
And swollen, red fingers.
The sons were on pins and needles
Impatiently grating their teeth till they hurt.
But the "old mule" did
His thing: he counted; wet
His red finger in his mouth;
Slowly, cautiously, felt every bill
Until at last he had it right. Later,
He portioned out the paper money to the group.
He stuffed the rest into a purse,
The purse into a canvas bag,
The bag deep, deep within his bosom, then straightening,
He slapped the nearest one on the back:
"Now, kids, let's go."
                              So they went,
Until they finally came to the bar.
Steam, as from a bathhouse, hit them in the face.
And there was a tremendous hubbub in the air;
Plates and glasses clattered;
The doors, spitting out and swallowing up people,

Never stopped for a second;
The strong smoke of pipes irritated
The smarting eyes and throats.
The electric lamps, small and distant,
Swayed through the haze as if floating.
The men ate hungrily and voraciously,
And they drank even more than they ate.
The old man was in high spirits,
His red face framed by his wet beard.
He winked, mischievously and slyly,
Poking Joe with his elbow,
Feeling his bosom every second.
And Joe felt both sad and cheerful;
His head was spinning from the beer,
And the noise and commotion made him sleepy.

Later, they brought cards to the table.
At first, the men were restrained, quiet,
But later they became hotly excited.
The beer glasses were continuously filled,
They stopped joking and teasing.
Obsessed, they sat silent,
Eyes angry and glaring. They played.
Young Walt's blood was boiling.
On the outside, he looked cold,
His face somewhat paler than usual;
But under the quiet, pale mask
He was as agitated as a running stream under ice.
His hate for the old man seethed,
For the sly, stingy man who, refusing to die,
Throws him a few base dollars
For all his blood and sweat during the long hard year.
Walt drank without stopping.
The further he was in the game, the more he lost.
And there sits that old devil with the Jew,
Oblivious, self-confident,
Slapping his fine son-in-law on the back.
The Jew will inherit everything,
Bag and baggage, nothing less. It's all the Jew's fault.
Because of the Jew his marriage fell through;
His girl laughed at him.
He could have been like everybody, a man among men,
Not dependent on the old devil.

And now the Jew will grab everything.
The edge of his cheeks flushed,
His mouth pressed together—one thin string,
His sharp little eyes narrowed,
Became cutting and red, shot through
With poisonous blood. Unfortunately, Joe
Had to joke about a false move
By the young Walt . . .
                                    And before they knew it
Walt laced into the Jew,
Pounding him in the face and chest
With huge iron-strong fists,
Kicking him with swift, thick boots.
He wouldn't let go of his victim, pounding away.
Heavy sounds reverberated in the thick damp air.
Suddenly there was a big outcry,
The whole house came running,
But before they could tear Walt away,
Joe already lay on the ground, half-dead,
His face no longer recognizable, black.
And in the corner of his twitching mouth
A pinkish-white stream
Of blood and foam formed.
                                    He never came to.
For three days he lay in the hospital,
Tottering on the brink of life and death.
The borderline was a pink and white cloud.
Looking within himself, he saw
His whole strange life, foreign and familiar.
He saw himself a child in a distant little town,
His mother in the bright summer pink
Hurries after him with gliding steps
And presses him to her heart, and murmurs: Yusl.
And then darkness, and again pinkness.
The *kheder,* rabbi, and friends—and the sea,
A wide, wavy, pink sea.
A new world, the new city, the hills,
The big, flabby fat Gentile girl.
A little red face with white hair
Who plays with the black dog; da-da.
Where did he see it? And through the long
Quiet, pink eternity,
He heard familiar voices as through walls

Of thick water: it seems it's his uncle,
And now it seems his aunt speaks, now his Gentile.
But little by little the pink light
Was extinguished; the pink cloud
Dissolved into infinity,
Sounds and colors were extinguished.

. . . It was a gray afternoon
When they gave Yusl a Jewish burial.
There were ten Jews. The aunt cried,
And the uncle said *kaddish* at the grave;
And the Gentile farm girl, the child in her arms,
Made the sign of the cross at the grave, and cried to the wind.

1921

Kentucky

Kentucky

*I*t seems somewhere still clangs a chain,
  And the wheeze of a whip's in the air,
And a man's howling mad like a hound . . .

Someone's grinding his teeth in his pain,
From his eyes anguish and hatred flare,
And warm blood drips from his wound.

But overhead shimmers a bright sun
Upon the trees covered with blossoms,
Upon the street which is clean and bright,

Upon the faces black as iron.
And the gentle south wind caresses
And carries not a whisper of hate.

                                    1918

George Washington

George Washington

A. Saturday Night

*W*hen George gets his weekly pay
      He first goes back to the barn
To say "Good-bye until Monday" to the donkeys.
He smells the fresh hay
And the pungent warmth of the horses.
The large barn is full and joyfully alive.
No doubt those clever horses understand
That tomorrow is free of lash and load.
Their pink mouths work with gusto,
Their big yellow teeth grind the oats,
Their moist nostrils flutter and steam,
Tickled by the fragrant hay.
The donkeys stand, pointed ears upright,
Tails switching, mouths grinding.
George engages them in a long conversation,
Drives a strange horse away from their oats,
And strokes their coarse, short haired fur.
Outside, George breaks into song,
First, because, he is by nature always cheerful,
Second, it is Saturday after work,
And, third, a bit of money excites him,
Short-lived as it is. So he sings out loud,
Intricate, ingenuous, rhythmic Negro songs,
Trilling the highest notes,

With nuance, stress, turn, and gesture.
Two or three blacks gather round.
A youth, catching the tune,
Starts to blow on a comb,
And suddenly George breaks into a dance.

George executes the dance thus: the earth
Starts to burn under his feet,
The whole of George suddenly and unexpectedly becomes
One fiery ball of nerves.
George seems to stand on one spot and fly.
Except for the tapping of his feet on the ground,
One would think that he is floating in the air
Suspended on invisible wires.
The circle claps its large black hands,
The Negro drools and blows on the comb
And looks like he'll burst from the strain.
George keeps time with his hands and feet,
With every limb of his quivering body.
His red mouth smiles from ear to ear,
His even white teeth sparkle,
His large eyes become larger,
The whites laced with small red veins.
His cast-iron-colored face
Starts to shine, the circle round him
Claps heatedly with all its strength,
And hums in ecstasy:
Hi-ha, hi-ha, hi-ha-he.

The dance over, George goes off
Through small side streets to the neighborhood
Where Hebrew Moses has a second-hand business.
George is about to redeem his Sunday clothes
Which he pawns regularly every Monday.
He knows from experience that he dares
Not play too much with money—it is round.
He gets a warm "How-do-you-do."
The small, bird-like eyes of Mose
Start to dance like little mice,
His sleepy face gets ever brighter,
And from a pile of old things and rotten shoes,
Mose sings out: Hallelujah shokh:
(Hallelujah from hello, from Negro—*shokher,*

From *shokher—shokh*). George smiles cheerfully
And counts the dollars into Mose's hand.
Mose ties up the Sunday finery,
Escorts the *shokh* out the door
And gives him a blessing for a good week.
And now George is transformed into a pilgrim.

That is, he starts home to his wife, to Maggie.
But, the devil take it, on the way there are
So many convivial places
To visit, that a man
Has to be made of iron not to be tempted.
On every corner, in every house
Attractive lamps shine
From red curtained doors and windows.
Banjos strum and call, and good brothers,
Wrapped in blue clouds of smoke,
Sit expansively around tables
And let themselves go in honor of Sunday.
They play cards and throw dice.
The foam of beer and the smell of whiskey rises
And mixes with the smell of barns.

In fact, the game isn't played for the pot.
The one who loses
Must treat the crowd to a round of drinks.
So it goes, around and around. The less the money
The more cheerful and happy, George.
His forehead shines, his eyes gleam,
His mouth doesn't close for one minute,
His tongue is loose and quips good humoredly.
The beer is cold, the whiskey burns.
It's a pity the night disappears so quickly.
The streets become silent and dead,
And when the last bar closes
George finally goes home.

His home is far from the city,
Among other shacks
Which lean against old, deserted barns.
The walls are crooked and rotted through,
The windows come up from the ground,
The roof has holes. Late in autumn,

When the rains come, Maggie complains
That she is afraid she'll float away.
At that George says that he has no such luck.
He has never seen an elephant swimming
Nor has he heard of such a thing. Maybe, says he,
She is a hippopotamus—the hippo cow
Can, indeed, swim. Says Maggie: if she
Were a hippo, she first would swallow
Such a nigger and then spit him out.
A respectable hippo, says she, would not take
His flesh into her mouth. George laughs good-naturedly.
Maggie, laughing, shakes her heavy body,
And goes into a fit of screeching.
Her black face gleams, her teeth shine,
Her eyes twinkle knowingly with pleasure,
Her heavy earrings jangle,
The thin crooked walls shake,
The chairs and table shake,
And the roof does its thing—it leaks.

When George concludes his long journey home,
He learns that Maggie has been waiting for him.
She has such a rotten habit. Saturday night
She first must have an accounting,
Even though she knows the precise account beforehand.
His arrival into the house takes place thus:
He cautiously opens the door and listens
He pokes his head in and draws it quickly back
As if he were afraid that something hard
Might unexpectedly fly at him.
If the enemy sits cheerfully—in a good mood,
Stroking the cat who dozes in her lap,
And the children
Are snoring peacefully in their beds,
George pushes in his package of clothes
And then appears full length in the door.
His eyes dance restlessly into every corner,
His mouth is stretched into a smile,
And this kind of dialogue takes place:
Maggie:
Good evening, nigger. Did you bring the pants?
George: (Silent and smiling)
Maggie:

No doubt he brought all sorts of goodies in the package:
A fat hen, a little whiskey
So his wife can have a little fun. No?
Ah! George knows very well
One can't make a meal out of Sunday pants,
How come he is so early today?
George:
He thought he heard
The first rooster crowing, and that's enough.
Maggie:
If Massa Lincoln were to come here,
He would lead that nigger to the middle
Of the market, tie him to a pole,
And would skin his black hide.
She would watch and be glad.
George:
Among decent folk, when a man comes home
Saturday night from work, the house is festive:
The table is set, the fat hen roasted,
The greens and sweet potatoes cooked,
The wife is happy and good to her man—
But in this house, hell-fire burns.

Now Maggie, restrained, softens.
Before she has time to speak her mind,
George, her man, is in a deep sleep.

B. A Weekday Sermon

*T*he passionate service was in progress.
     In the small church, half sunken into the ground,
The low ceiling sweated,
As did the dirty, blue-painted walls
And colored glass windows.
The flames of gas lights and candles
Flickered pale and fluttered.
A thick hot haze floated in the air
Smelling of sweat, whiskey, perfume,
Of horses, chickens, paint and incense.
Hot, the brothers with their hair cut to the scalp
Threw their coats off,
The make-up of the sisters ran,

Snaking in red lines,
Striping their faces and necks outlandishly.
Man, wife, and child sang.
White teeth shone
From reddish gums.
Large eyes stared wildly,
Rolling ecstatically to the ceiling.
High cheekbones and stubborn foreheads
Burned in shades of cast-iron, bronze, and copper.
In the low house,
The song surged out, passionate and fervent:

> Give me that old time religion,
> Give me that old time religion,—
> It's good enough for me.
>
> It's good for the children of Israel
> It's good for the children of Israel—
> And it's good enough for me.
>
> It was good for Paul and Silas,
> It was good for Paul and Silas—
> And it's good enough for me.
>
> It's good when the world is burning,
> It's good when the world is burning—
> And it's good enough for me.
>
> It's good in the hour of dying,
> It's good in the hour of dying—
> And it's good enough for me.
>
> So give me that old time religion,
> Give me that old time religion—
> It's good enough for me.

They sang this song in ecstasy,
Ever louder, stronger, more heatedly.
Once finished, they began again
With more zeal and more rapture.
Singing thus, they went into a dance.
A hot mass of singing flesh
In one big ball of passion
Unbraided itself and came together,
Hands on shoulders, chest to chest,
Breath eager and heavy,
Eyes tightly shut, ecstatic,
Half awake, half slumbering in the haze.

210

The earrings and bracelets of the wives
Sounded heavy and sensual,
The red lips burning, pleading,
And the nostrils excited, trembling.
Later they sang another song,
Another song—haunting and soft:

> Oh, Mary, don't ya weep, don't ya mourn,
> Oh, Mary, don't ya weep, don't ya mourn,
> Pharoah's army got drowned,
> Oh, Mary don't ya weep.
>
> Oh, how I long to be far from here,
> To stand on that hill where Moses stood,
> Pharoah's army is drowned,
> Oh, Mary don't ya weep.
>
> Far, far away, I see like in a dream
> Angels floating on a cherry tree.
> Pharoah's army is drowned,
> Oh, Mary don't ya weep.

And when it came to the words:
"Dig my grave with a shovel of gold,
Let me down with golden chains."
The fervor grew
So that tears ran from their cheeks,
And people sobbed joyfully.
Others fell down,
Beating their heads on the floor, eyes glazed,
White foam around their black mouths,
Striking their chests with all their strength,
Bursting into a roaring song:

> Dig my grave with a shovel of gold,
> Let me down with golden chains
> Pharoah's army is drowned—
> Oh, Mary don't ya weep!

C. Thomas

*W*hen Brother George and Sister Maggie
Again breathed the outdoor air,
They walked quietly and piously at first.

The sky was clear and starry,
The late summer breeze caressed them,
The leafy trees talked to one another,
And crickets chirped confidently.
A glass of beer would sure suit George's
Dry, parched throat.
If Maggie were not here, he would certainly
Have ducked into an open tavern.
But what can one do? She walks along and puffs
And hangs on his arm, whistling and panting.
A real locomotive, thinks George.
And his heart fills with regret.
He thinks of Brother Thomas
Shining, perfumed, dressed-up
In a shirt with large red stripes.
And he feels like fainting.
He hawks, spits, and starts to hum,
First to himself, then louder.
In a roundabout way
He asks naively why
The church needs people
Who have no religion in their hearts?
He says: Take Brother Thomas, for instance.
That nigger comes into church, not to pray,
But to lead the women astray.
He parades around idly, doesn't want to work,
Sponges off of another husband's table.
That nigger, he said, should be lynched.
Why doesn't the nigger marry
And get his own wife?
Then he wouldn't need to stare his eyes out
And pinch other men's women in church.
No one can fool him. He sees.
Maggie says casually:
First of all, Thomas didn't pinch her.
No one pinches her in church, she goes there to pray.
But if her nigger sees such things,
Then it's a sure sign
That he, himself, has no religion.
A man who comes to church to pray
Must look into the Book, and not
At another man's hands. Now George gets angry:
Religion here, religion there, he says.

212

Thomas could be a saint like Saint John—
But if that nigger crosses his threshold
When he, George Washington, is not at home,
Then he, George, will break both of his legs.
He'll leave his hands whole
So that that black son of a bitch will be able
To play fiddle in the market.
As for the Pharaoh's fat cow—Maggie, that is—
The long whip will do.
As it serves for his donkeys
So will it certainly serve for her.

But Thomas was not very frightened.
He depended on his legs
And was confident that they would
Carry him safely away from any danger.
If George should knock on a front door, there is a back door.
A fence is made to jump over.
No need to bear a grudge—
What a man says in the heat of passion is unimportant.
Thomas is not eager to work.
Quite the reverse. He says a man is not a donkey,
But if a nigger wants to go into the harness,
He can suit himself. Thomas says
He would rather make out as is.
So wherever there is a husband who works,
Thomas hangs around his wife—
But only when the man is not at home.
Today, Maggie—tomorrow, Peggy—or whoever.
To them, Thomas is a most welcome guest
Because, for one thing, he is a virile youth.
He is spicy and saucy and sharp.
When he starts to imitate people—
Two Negroes arguing in the tavern,
George driving and talking to the donkeys,
The Reverend banging his belly in the church—
He conjures them up as if in the flesh,
As if one were there and saw them.
In addition, Thomas has another virtue:
He likes to pay for a favor.
And the house which he visits
Is as full of good things as an eye socket.
When Thomas walks around on the outskirts of the city,

He doesn't forget to take his bag.
He doesn't let any grass grow under his feet
As he passes through, walking. If there is an apple tree
Too close to the fence, Thomas is not lazy.
He shakes the tree. The same goes
For pears, for apricots, for sour cherries.
As if he were the owner, he digs up potatoes,
A beet, an onion, a head of cabbage.
If a hen or a duck wanders,
She finds her peace in Thomas' bag.
And so it goes. Considering the abundance of Kentucky,
Thomas jokes that
He could support a dozen wives,
Not only one.
George, however, was not impressed
By Thomas and his seven virtues.
He became as stubborn as a mule:
He doesn't want Thomas in his house,
He doesn't want his favors—and that's that.
As he sees it, that nigger is just a coward.
Some trick, says George, for a man to have swift feet.
A rabbit is faster than that nigger.
How come, he asks, he doesn't stop
And doesn't want to listen to George's words
So that he knows once and for all how things stand.
So Thomas sends word: It's not necessary.
He knows where he stands,
And he doesn't want any arguments
With a person he feels close to.
Maggie says: The nigger is going crackers.
His black skin doesn't know when it's well off.
The nigger deserves to be whipped
Until his foolishness is knocked out of his head.

D. Thanksgiving

*I*t rained the whole day.
A biting cold drizzle
Kept sifting from a low, cloudy, gray sky.
A sheet of ice covered the asphalt pavement
And George's harnessed donkeys
Slipped more than walked.

The dampness pierced his bones,
The wind angrily lashed his face.
The whip was cold and frozen
And slipped like a snake from his hand.

After the hard day,
George, frozen, fell into the house—
He stopped on the threshold, stock still,
The coal stove was burning—blazing:
One big, red, fiery piece of coal.
The house was steamy.
His nostrils inhaled
The hot, sharp smells of a roast.
The first thing that hit his eyes
Was the table, covered with an ironed cloth,
Loaded with and smelling of all sorts of good things.
The turkey smelled luscious,
The golden brown skin sparkling
With clear drops of fat, like pearls,
Whole rabbits, as if alive,
As if caught jumping,
Were surrounded by brown potatoes
And crisp greens.
The tart cranberry juice
Made his mouth water.
Large red apples and oranges
In a wicker basket
Spread a cool odor in the heat.
Bottles of beer, necks outstretched,
Like soldiers in a line,
Peeked out of chipped ice
From a laundry basket on the floor.

Before George could come to his senses
Something pulled at his heart
And he remained standing, frightened.
On the couch near the clean covered table,
Their eyes shining brightly,
Their curly-wire heads bouncing,
The children played with Uncle Thomas.
The nigger sits dressed-up and perfumed,
Innocent as the day is long, rolling his eyes.
Involuntarily, George jumped back.

He thinks they are going to trick him.
But at this point, Maggie, flushed and shining,
Paddled out like a ship, approached smiling
With her teeth and pink eyes:
If Brother Thomas, showing his kindness,
Brought so many good things into the house—
Then it is no more than right—she thinks,
That he also should enjoy everything.
Anyway, why put on airs?
A man is not a peacock. It's about time
For a reconciliation.
Here Thomas spoke up:
He doesn't know any rhyme or reason
Why brothers should quarrel.
He has enough enemies, he says.
So what? Angry tongues clatter.
As it is written in the Holy Book,
"A two-edged sword is their tongue." He says
He has for a long time wanted to come to George,
To open his eyes, so that George can see
That he, Thomas, is his friend. And as for
All these good things on the table,
Maggie should do him a favor and
Not make a big fuss over it. It's not even
Worth mentioning. He doesn't want money.
And further, he gets these things for nothing.
In fact, he brought
Some white folks' moonshine so that
They could drink a toast to brotherhood
And let there be peace in the world.
George thought:
That nigger is flattering me too much.
He's playing possum, he wants to fool me.
But so far, I'm the boss here . . .
First of all, let's eat.
So they sat down at the magnificent table,
Drank some whiskey,
Clinked glasses, smacked their lips,
And started to gorge themselves.
The whole house echoed with the sound
Of plates, knives, and teeth.
The stripped bones flew to the cat
On the ground. Large drops of sweat

216

Stood out on their necks and foreheads,
And faces shone as if they were polished.
When the initial hunger was satisfied, they
Rinsed it all down with foaming, chilled beer,
Clinked whiskey glasses again,
And started eating once more.
George became more sympathetic,
And Thomas poured out
His sorrowful heart. He knows, he says,
That his is not a life,
Even a dog has a bit of a home,
But he, oh, he drags himself around, a wanderer,
And has no roof over him.
Where is the limit, he asks, to his suffering?
Maybe George knows of a girl for him—
A good, quiet girl. Money doesn't matter.
The most important thing for him is a quiet home
Where, on Sunday, he can sit by his fire
And read the holy word of the Bible.
And Thomas quietly puts his head down
And starts to cry like a baby.

Meanwhile, little by little, the sleepy children
Go off to their corners.
Outdoors, the wet wind whined,
Drumming with frozen rain
On the roof and in the small windowpanes.
The stove crackled, and blue smoke
From their strong, odorous pipes
Curled and circled around the ceiling.
They kissed each other, comforted each other, cried,
And immediately had a fit of laughter.
And then they sang, heartily:
First, the spirited songs of the church,
Of hell and heaven and angels,
Of Holy Saint Peter, who stands
At the threshold of heaven, with a shining sword
And does not allow landowners in soft rocking chairs
To enter.
And then they
Sang long, sweet, slow melodies
Of tragic love and of Negro suffering.
The song of the lover who mourns

The young lynched "easy breezy John."
And the famous comic song of
"Horse and fly and two small mice,
Sit in a corner and play with dice."
And between songs,
They toasted each other and drank.
Their faces burned like fire,
Their eyes, hot and wild,
Glowed like hot living coals.

When finally the lamp went out,
And the loud lamenting quieted,
Only the hot stove crackled red,
Throwing red patches on the walls
And on curly black shadow-heads.
The house groaned with hot sounds,
With yearning, sighing, and moaning.
Shadows, caught in the roaring red haze,
Tossed as if in a fever.
And into the windows, the night looked,
Knocking with rain-fingers on the panes,
Whistling with resounding screaming winds.
And it put the red haze to sleep.

December, 1920

The Silk Shirt

The Silk Shirt

*T*om had a shirt of heavy silk
  And everybody was jealous.
The red stripe blinded the eye,
Its richness radiated with every twist.
Whenever Tom came into church at night,
Many another's wife was brought
To sinful thoughts in God's house.
But Thomas didn't concern himself with that.
He unbuttoned his coat as if by accident
So that the silk was more noticeable.
Husbands scowled and looked angry,
Their blood boiled.
They cursed Thomas, wishing he'd break every bone,
While standing in his flashing shirt, all alone.

Once Thomas, in an unfortunate hour,
Pawned the shirt with Hebrew Mose.
One week, two, a third went by—
The orphaned shirt hung on a nail.
The deadline was now long over due,
And the subject hangs, not knowing what to do.
The shirt hangs, forsaken and alone.
Mose cursed Thomas's every bone.
It seems as if the Negro ran out of the earth,
Drank up his money, is not seen or heard,
And then, George ducked into the store . . .

Smelled here, smelled there, fingered more,
Recognized old Thomas's shirt, and glowed.
Once and for all, he'll get back what is owed.
And have something to boast about to his wife
And at the same time give Thomas some strife.
George pretended that he was, as it were, indifferent
To vain things, mocked them,
Laughed heartily at his own clever words,
And suddenly grabbed Mose quite unexpectedly,
Just when Mose thought George was bothering him for
    nothing.
With disdain, George felt the shirt from top to bottom:
For instance, how much is this rag worth?
To Mose's astonishment, as soon as George
Heard the price, he didn't think twice,
Didn't bargain, paid on the spot.
Mose was amazed: What the hell
Is the matter with that nigger tonight?
Maybe there is something that he swiped.

Meanwhile, God helped Thomas.
He became prosperous during the week,
And as soon as he felt a bit of mint,
He hied himself to Mose
To redeem his good shirt. With great aplomb,
Tom went into Mose's store,
And before Mose could open his mouth
Tom was already jumping like a rubber ball.
Dancing here, dancing there, and singing a song:
"The great day is coming, it comes, it comes.
It's riding on a cloud, and the cloud is red,
To the saint it brings life, to the villain death—
The great day is coming, it comes, it comes."
Mose thought: A holiday for the *shokh*!
He's going to get it.
In the meantime, Tom doesn't stand on one spot.
Now he is here, now there,
He dances around the store. That young man
Shakes the walls with his song and dance . . .
The *shokh* in front, and behind him Mose,
Who tells him the truth straight from the heart:
The story is simple—short and sweet.
A moth climbed into the shirt

And wrought disaster, hole on hole—
(Mose quickly worked in: You should live so long, *shokh*!)
Fortunately he, Mose, in the nick of time,
Found a customer for the shirt.
Thomas abruptly stopped,
As if he had lost his breath.
One could clearly see: His skin gets pale,
One leg, in mid-jig is frozen in the air.
Now Mose comforts him a bit,
Moralizes a bit: What can one expect—
An unsettled person—a person who goes ahead
And pawns a good silk shirt,
And we never see him or hear from him—
What's to be done? A moth is a moth.

That same evening, with a broken spirit,
Tom was sitting in church, tired and weary,
This time tightly buttoned.
The brothers sat with bowed heads,
The Reverend droned on, monotonously and long,
And Tom was bored and regretful.
His heart gnawed and ached,
He couldn't get the shirt out of his mind.
Thomas looked neither to the right or to the left,
His teary eyes were glued to the book.
But when people got up to go home,
He saw how George was showing his teeth,
And the red stripe hit him in the eye.
Tom, as if convulsed, went blue, then pale,
Before he knew it, George had disappeared
And Thomas remained alone with his wrath.
For the first time, he delved the secret from inside:
That nigger George took him for a ride.

Thomas left for the bar, his heart bitter.
The world was melancholy and black.
The brothers didn't even recognize Thomas,
So pitiful and wretchedly sad.
It took more than one good drink
To drive out the melancholy
And instill some life in the young man,
To help him again see the world in a rose-colored light.
Only then did his mouth open.

He drew a breath and felt himself free.
Heatedly, he expounded fully
On the perfidy which burns and poisons,
On people's falseness and pettiness, on the self-interest
Which pays back goodness with stones.
Without pondering too long, he immediately
Went into a racy joke, laughed,
Mocked the Reverend, and slapped his knee.
The crowd nearly died laughing.
Tom jingled the last of his silver,
The price of the red striped shirt, in his hand.

And later, when the bar closed,
Thomas dragged himself into the black night.
The ground swayed like water in the wind,
And Thomas waged war with the dogs.
Staggering, falling from his feet,
But watching out for holes, somehow,
He walked and sang, walked and hummed:
"The great day is coming, it comes, it comes.
It is riding on a cloud, and the cloud is red.
To the saint it brings life, and to the villain death."

May, 1921

224

The End of Thomas

The End of Thomas

A. Hunger

*H*unger started to gnaw at him.
    At first, suffering from fear and remorse,
Thomas didn't dare move.
He lay with his head rolled into his belly,
Covered with dead leaves and branches,
His sharp ears alert as a dog's,
Trembling at the slightest rustle from the woods.
But as the hunger grew stronger,
It drove Thomas from his hiding place.
His black head with its close-cut hair
Poked out more often
From the yellow and green rustling cover.
His eyes, no longer pink but bloody red,
Seemed to pop out of his head.
His face was distorted, not shining black, but gray,
His teeth—white, pointed.
His head looked like an animal's,
An animal of an unknown kind.
Luckily, the weather was mild,
As sometimes happens in the middle of winter.
Here and there the snow was seen.
During the day, a mild winter sun
Warmed the bare trees,
The dead, thin branches on the ground,

And the hole, Thomas's hiding place.
Squirrels jumping around,
Stopped to look at the head,
But would not come close to him.
Under more leisurely circumstances, Thomas could
Make them dance on his shoulders.
But here, as if in spite, they wouldn't move.
He tried to lure them with his hands,
Called them with a muffled voice,
Enticed them with his lips, but the squirrels
Kept away from him.
It could be they were frightened by the bodiless head,
Or by the unnatural, hoarse voice,
Or by the murderous look in his eyes.
But whatever it was, the little devils
Kept their distance from him,
Holding their thick, gray tails high,
Jumping and climbing on the trees,
And playing charmingly. And the head
With its bloodshot, dull eyes,
Concentrated on those gray skins.

On the third day of his hiding
Thomas could no longer lie still.
It was as if an angry dog
Had entered his insides;
The dog gnawed with his teeth,
Pawed with sharp copper nails,
And tore out pieces of living flesh.
The dog drove him out of the woods.
Thomas wanted to fool the dog,
Tried to stuff his mouth with leaves,
Moist roots, pieces of thin branches,
But the dog didn't allow himself to be fooled.
He quieted down for a moment,
But when he tasted the bitterness,
The sour, cold bitterness
Which slid frostily, poisonously
Down his parched red-hot throat
Like a cold stream on hot limestone,
He got wilder
And started pawing more furiously.
And Thomas had to give in to him.

He knew the dog was driving him to his death.
If he sticks a foot out of the woods,
He will be bagged like a wild animal.
And he also knew that he couldn't
Count on any mercy.
At best, he would be lawfully
Sentenced to hang by his neck.
But he couldn't stop himself:
The hungry dog drove him,
And Thomas obeyed. He went.

B. Justice

*T*he large chamber of the courthouse
Was crowded, clogged, suffocating.
Justice was proceeding.
First they heard the unimportant cases:
A father sued his son for beating him up,
Two farmers argued over a field,
A young man was caught with whiskey.
The crowd was bored.
The old judge with soft checks,
Smooth gray hair, and new teeth
Didn't hurry at all. He sat
Solemnly, peacefully, on his broad bench,
Playing with his watch chain,
Letting his eyes stray to the ceiling.
They stopped for a moment on the walls
Where the revered fathers
Of the great republic hung:
George Washington, Jefferson, Lincoln.
Good naturedly, he smiled to them.
It was quiet. People talked
In half tones. The reporters' pens
Scratched quickly across the papers,
And the tall old-fashioned clock
Sleepily sounded: tic-toc, tic-toc.

As soon as they brought Tom in,
A hubbub arose in the chamber.
The soft, sleepy eyes of the mob
Suddenly revived,

Cold, sharp, menacing.
It seemed as if from every eye
Came a sharp, thin spear
Which stuck into the Negro's limbs,
Branding and burning his black skin.
Men clenched their teeth so hard
That their faces looked
Four-cornered and sharp, as if carved
With thin, tight, stone-chiseled mouths.
They brought the Negro to trial
Soon after he was caught in the field.
His blue coat was smeared
With half-dried wet clay and soil,
Covered with moss and wild brambles from the woods.
His shoes were twisted and scratched from the thorns.
The only thing which was presentable
Was the fine silk shirt.
His face was grayish-blue.
Around one eye, a bile as large as a fist,
Cried with heat. The other eye,
Like a red, driven mouse,
Ran around, over walls and heads,
Banging against thin, sharp objects,
And not finding a place to rest.

Little by little, he came to himself.
He quieted down in his seat.
The trial went quickly:
The jurors were chosen, in the hall
A quiet buzzing sounded.
The old judge spoke sedately
And Thomas forgot himself for a while,
As if he were pulled along by a current.
He eagerly looked at every move
Of every new juror,
Tried to look into the other's eyes.
His glance was feverish and quick,
Resting here and there on people
With whom he had permitted himself to joke.
This one, that one used to slap him on the back
Because of his clever proverb, or joke.
It all seemed a bad dream,
As if he were a spectator. He thought:

He really does not understand
How can one man coldly
Sentence another man to death.

When his eye felt
The steel, piercing looks,
And his ears heard the angry, impatient roar,
Coming from the street,
Reverberating on the walls of the courthouse
Like a cold, stormy wave,
His brain suddenly seemed on fire:
It was he, he, Thomas, who sits
And looks at his unavoidable, black fate,
That it is he who will pay with his skin.
Fearful anxiety seized him
And white drops of sweat, like large peas,
Ran from his black face.
His young, bubbling blood cried from pain.
He felt like bursting into a roar,
Like banging his head against a hard stone,
But his eye again met with another's,
And it was clear, anew,
That it could not, and would not, be different
The one eye finally rested.
It remained fixed on Lincoln's portrait,
Boring itself into the wrinkled face,
And stubbornly clinging to it.
From the depths of his heart, he cried: Father Lincoln
Have pity on a stray nigger!

1922

231

Appendix

Parting*

*T*he picture of my final parting from home
  Rises up before me with all its anguish
And excruciating pain: it's a mid-summer day—
The sun, at high noon, burns—burns;
The dahlia plant in our small garden,
My mother's pride, which she lovingly tends,
Languishes in the burning sun;
The broad red-leaved bouquets
Droop their heads, powerless. My mother cries
And grieves in her sorrow, as if in mourning—
I am saying good-bye forever to my home.
Just as one leads a small child by the hand,
My father takes me by the hand and leads me
To the small, old, familiar synagogue.
We go quietly, with small steps, carefully—
Mount three-four steps
To the women's section, cut across,
Descend three-four steps into the synagogue,
Pass the platform facing east,
Stop by the pulpit, near the Ark.
The synagogue is quiet and cool and shadowy,

---

*This poem is from *Yunge Yurn.* The text I used for my translation appears in *Amerika in Yidishn Vort,* ed. N. Mayzel (New York: Yiddisher Kultur Farband, 1955), pp. 377–378.

The light dim; it is quiet and shadowy.
My father holds me by the hand. He stands
Slightly bent and his shoulders twitch.
I look at him from a side; for the first time
I notice: my father has grown old.
His fine beard—almost entirely white,
His forehead—creased with deep lines,
His strained eyes—full of sorrow.
My father speaks in a broken voice,
Stops himself in the middle, starts speaking again
In a whisper, his voice breaking; the whole time
He does not let my hand out of his.
And I—I am afraid to raise my eyes—
I would break out into tears
In the solemn stillness of the old synagogue.
A few years later, in the turmoil of New York,
When I once again relived
Those painful moments of parting,
I tried to preserve that moment
Of short, whispered phrases—
I will end my song with them:
"To me, generations cried:
. . . My child, remain a Jew.
Let your father's inheritance and suffering
Be guarded deep in your heart.
I was not cursed with gold,
But God endowed me with a spirit;
He does not withhold His mercy from us.
I carry generations upon generations in my heart—
I am tired, I am old, you are young—
Go forth, God protects my child;
Let your soul remain pure
In spite of the temptations of life and sin.
Do not forget our journey in the world.
Be a Jew!" . . . —He spoke no more;
But his eyes sparkled, shone,
With faith in his quiet plea.
In the synagogue, the eternal light flickered
With its quivering, sad flame.
With awe and anxiety, I bowed
And wrapped my face in the curtain of the Ark.

1951
I. J. Schwartz

Glossary

aleph First letter of the Hebrew alphabet.

caftan Long overcoat traditionally worn by observant Jews.

Eyn yankev A collection of Talmudic legends and homilies.

hakofes The carrying of the Torah amidst the congregation during the holiday of *Simkhas Torah*.

hallah White bread traditionally eaten on the Sabbath.

havdalah Ceremony to say good-bye to the Sabbath and to greet the new week.

kheder Hebrew religious school for young boys.

kaddish Prayer for the dead.

kiddish Benediction over the wine.

kishka Cow's intestines stuffed with pudding.

kugel Pudding.

lekhayim A toast which means "to life."

lulev Palm branch.

mazuma Cash (from the Yiddish mezumen).

mezuzah Small tube containing an inscribed strip of parchment attached to the doorpost of premises occupied by observant Jews, and symbolically kissed by persons entering or leaving.

Midrash A body of post-Talmudic literature of Biblical exegesis.

minyen Prayer quorum of ten male adults.

Mishna A collection of post-Biblical laws and rabbinical discussions of the Second Century B.C., which forms part of the Talmud.

mizrekh A fixture on the east wall of an Orthodox household, often in the form of a Palestinian scene, to mark the direction in which Jerusalem lies.

Oleynu The last prayer of the service before the mourner's *kaddish*.

shma-Yisroel Hear O Israel.

shokh Chess.

shokher Black.

sholem aleykhem A greeting Jews extend to each other. Literally means "Peace be with you." Equivalent to hello.

shoykhet Ritual slaughterer.

Simkhas Torah Holiday celebrating completion of year's reading cycle of the Torah scrolls.

tallith Prayer shawl.

Yiddishkayt A way of life that totally encompasses Jewish language, traditions, and beliefs.

Bibliography

Books and Translations by Schwartz

Hamlet and Julius Caesar. Translation. New York, *Forward,* 1918.
Kentoki. New York: M. N. Mayzel, 1925.
Undzer lid fun Shpanya. Translation. New York: Yiddish Kultur Gezelshaft, 1931.
Chaim Nachman Bialik, lider un poemen. Translation. Michigan: Natsionaler Arbiter Farband, 1935.
Hebreyeshe poesye. Translation. New York: Yidish Natsyonaler Arbiter Farband, 1942.
Khaim Nakhman Bialik-Shriftn, Yidish. Edited Volume. New York: Yidish Natsyonaler Arbiter Farband, 1946.
Seyfer Ha Shabat. Translation. New York: Yidish Natsyonaler Arbeter Farband, 1947.
Yunge yorn. Mexico: Yidish Tsentral Comitet, 1952.
Fun undzer oytser. Translation. New York: Cyco, 1953.
Geklibene lider. New York: Yidish Natsyonaler Arbeter Farband, 1961.
Shirat Kentoki. Translation into Hebrew. Jerusalem: Bialik Institute, 1962.
Lider un poemen. Tel Aviv: *Di goldene keyt,* 1968.

Works about Schwartz and *Kentucky*

(All of these works are in Yiddish except for the articles by Dubrovsky, Jones, and Zaltz.)
Auerbach, Ephraim. "Y. Y. Shvartz." *Der tog-morgan dzhornal* (April 25, 1965).
Blum, Israel. "In Mayn Literarishe Akhsanye." *Zukunft* (January 1961): 30–36.
Dubrovsky, Gertrude. "The Americanization of 'The Grandchildren of Wander.' " *Judaism* (Spring 1974): 216–27.

————. "Between a Yiddish Poet and His Translator." *Yiddish* (Winter/Spring 1976): 67–107.

————. "Kentucky's Yiddish Poet." Magazine. *The Courier-Journal and Times* (September 14, 1975): 25–29.

————. "I. J. Schwartz (1885–1971) In Memoriam." *Midstream* (December 1971): 52–57.

————. "I. J. Schwartz's *Kentucky.*" *Jewish Currents* (June 1984): 12–38.

————. "A Jew in the Southland: I. J. Schwartz's *Kentucky.*" *Conservative Judaism* 26 (Spring 1972): 33–39.

————. "In Search of America: Lexington, Ky. and Farmingdale, N.J." *Midstream* (October 1988): 29–33.

Eisland, Reuben. "Y. Y. Shvarts in Kentoki." *Der indzl* (August 1925): 6–13.

Glants-Leyeles, Aaron. "Literarishe Memuaren." *Di goldene keyt* 39: 141–143.

————. "Shvartz, Der Amerikaner." *Zukunft* (December 1961): 468–469.

————. "Y. Y. Shvarts, dikhter un iberzetser." *Der tog-morgen dzhornal* (November 16, 1957).

Glatstein, Jacob. *In tokh genumen: 1948–1956.* New York: Farband, 1956: 261–266.

Jones, Joseph R. "I. J. Schwartz in Lexington." *The Kentucky Review* 3 (1981): 23–40.

Kana, F. "Y. Y. Shvarts: Kentoki." *Der Oyfkum* (January 1927): 3–11.

Kominski, Yehoshua. "Kentoki fun Y. Y. Shvarts." *Workmen's Circle Year Book.* New York: Workmen's Circle, 1945: 40–41.

Lev, Avrom. "Y. Y. Shvarts." *Lebns fragen* (Nov-Dec, 1968)

Meisel, Nachman. "Y. Y. Shvarts' bukh kentoki." *Literarishe bleter.* N. 127. Warsaw (October 8, 1926): 670–671.

Mukdoni, A. "Tsvey yubeleyn." *Di goldene keyt* 24 (November 24, 1956): 155–165.

Niger, Shmuel. "Amerikaner yidishe lider." *Der tog* (May 10, 1925).

————. "An amerikaner yidishe familya." *Der tog* (May 5, 1925): 3.

————. "Kentoki fun Y. Y. Shvarts." *Der tog* (N. D., 1921).

————. "Y. Y. Shvarts: tsu zayn drayfakhign yubeley." *Der tog* (January 1, 1956).

Pat, Jacob. "Y. Y. Shvarts: tsu sayn 75 yubeley." *Di presse* (November 19, 1961).

Reisen, Zalman. *Leksicon fon der yidisher literatur.* Vilna, 1929.

Ribalov, Moshe. "Naye erd." *Zukunft* (February 1927): 184–186.

Shatski, Jacob. "Kentoki fon Y. Y. Shvarts." *Kultur* (October 9, 1925): 5/10.

Shender, M. "Faryidisht a yidn." *Di yidishe tsaytung* (January 8, 1958).

Steinberg, Noah. "Y. Y. Shvarts." *Yidish amerike.* New York, 1929. 121–147.

Shulman, Elias. "Y. Y. Shvarts: 1885–1971." *Der veker* (January 1972): 8–12.

Tverski, A. "Di groyse balade fon umet." *Zukunft* (November 1953): 44–46.

Vaynper, Zishe. *Yidishe shriftshteler.* Vol. II. New York: Posy-Shoulson Press, 1936: 131–139.

Yeshurin, Yefim. "Y. Y. Shvarts-Bibliografye." *Y. Y. Shvarts. A. Raboy: pionern in Amerika.* Buenos Aires: Ateneo Literario En El Iwo, 1964: 299–305.

Zaltz, F. *Our Eternal Culture.* Winnipeg: Universal Press, 1956: 195–221.

Zinger, S. "Vegn shrayber un kikher: Y. Y. Shvarts." *Undzer veg* (January 1962): 15–17.

————. "Y. Y. Shvarts." *Forward* (October 31, 1971) Section 2: 10/14.